"This book is a gift to anyone who reads it. It's like sitting down with your best friend, who happens to be incredibly wise and vulnerable and knows deep truths about Jesus. I've been lucky enough to have Laney as a best friend for years now, and I'm so thankful for the truth she has spoken over me, and now I'm so excited for y'all to get to experience that for yourselves. I have to be honest; at times I forgot I was reading my best friend's book and thought I was reading one from a life-long author who just happened to be sharing such relatable stories. Sit down, grab a cup of coffee with coconut creamer like Laney would, and dive into this life-changing message!"

Sadie Robertson Huff, best-selling author, speaker, and Founder of Live Original

"I've known Laney since we were both young girls and have loved seeing her journey to follow God's voice and heed His call on her life. This book is a beautiful reflection of that. Relational. Empathetic. Encouraging. Timely. This is for every woman, every girl, every DAUGHTER — to learn or perhaps rediscover their identity and know just how loved and cherished they truly are by God."

Kari Jobe Carnes, GRAMMY-nominated and Dove Award-winning worship leader

"We have never read a book that made the amazing relationship we can experience with God more real, magnificent, and understandable. Laney Rene is supernaturally gifted by God to communicate not only what is on her heart but also what is on our Father's heart. This book will inspire you to become who you already are in Christ. You will begin to better understand how you can live in the manifest presence of our Father's glory, grace, power, and unconditional love. This is a must-read for everyone who desires to experience the fullness of life God freely offers. The fact that Laney is one of our five granddaughters is not why we shared how much this book will bless you. You won't be able to put this book down, and you won't be able to keep it from lifting you up."

James and Betty Robison, Hosts of LIFE TODAY TV
and Founders of LIFE Outreach International

Daughter

Becoming who you *already* are

LANEY RENE

BREAKFAST
FOR SEVEN

Daughter: Becoming Who You Already Are

Copyright © 2023 Laney Rene

Scripture quotations marked ESV are taken from the ESV® Bible (The Holy Bible, English Standard Version®), Copyright © 2001 by Crossway, a publishing ministry of Good News Publishers. Used by permission. All rights reserved.

Scripture quotations marked NASB are taken from the (NASB®) New American Standard Bible®, Copyright © 1960, 1971, 1977, 1995, 2020 by The Lockman Foundation. Used by permission. All rights reserved. lockman.org

Scripture quotations marked NIV are taken from the Holy Bible, New International Version®, NIV®, Copyright © 1973, 1978, 1984, 2011 by Biblica, Inc.™ Used by permission of Zondervan. All rights reserved worldwide. www.zondervan.com The "NIV" and "New International Version" are trademarks registered in the United States Patent and Trademark Office by Biblica, Inc.™

Scripture quotations marked NKJV are taken from the New King James Version®. Copyright © 1982 by Thomas Nelson. Used by permission. All rights reserved.

Scripture quotations marked NLT are taken from the *Holy Bible*, New Living Translation, Copyright © 1996, 2004, 2015 by Tyndale House Foundation. Used by permission of Tyndale House Publishers, Carol Stream, Illinois 60188. All rights reserved.

Scripture quotations marked TPT are taken from The Passion Translation®. Copyright © 2017, 2018, 2020 by Passion & Fire Ministries, Inc. Used by permission. All rights reserved. ThePassionTranslation.com.

ISBN: 978-1-951701-42-0 (Hardback)
ISBN: 978-1-951701-51-2 (eBook)
ISBN: 978-1-951701-80-2 (Audiobook)

Produced by Breakfast for Seven
breakfastforseven.com

Printed in the United States of America.

Contents

Introduction

I could feel the vibration of the drums. They were so loud, yet somehow I had gotten used to the sound and the feeling. As I knelt behind them before I went out on stage, I said under my breath and just to myself, "Laney, remember this moment." There was a line being drawn in the sand. This was a moment I knew I would look back on and remember what God had done. Though what was ahead was unknown and unexpected, I was the surest I had ever been about where I was going.

On a stage where I had moved through my tears and felt more desperate than I ever had before, I danced with freedom and celebration for one last dance. It was sweet — a bitter kind of sweet — but it was time, and I knew it.

After five more songs, I skated and danced to stage right. I slid down the stage ramp to meet my friend, who was always there waiting to help me get back up. From there, I went straight to the dressing room, got my stuff together, packed up, and headed back to the bus. It was the final night I would be crawling into my bunk, the last time I thought I might sleep on a tour bus, but I crawled in, and just like every other night before, I closed the curtain with an overwhelming peace and expectation.

Ahh . . . I could breathe. It was easy and light in there. Heavenly.

It was just a bunk on a tour bus; some people compare it to the size of a coffin, but it was the place where real love met me in a way I had never known before.

I had called my mom in that bunk just three months before and told her I would like to go to prison because, in my mind, prison seemed better than my current reality. I had cried more tears than I knew were physically possible in that bunk. I had asked questions, been upset, and hidden in that bunk. But most of all, I experienced His love for me in that bunk.

What started with heartbreak and a very desperate cry of "God, would you just hold me?" Turned into a story I could've never come up with on my own. A story of His faithfulness. A story of His redemption and a relentless love. I was being wooed, romanced, and divinely persuaded towards something — or rather, Someone — who was changing everything for me.

My prayer now is not that she would never ask the question, but that she will *always* know who to ask.

Chapter One
Who Am I?

One of the very first times I remember questioning my identity was when I was only five years old. My childhood best friend and I lived in the same neighborhood. We played every day together. And, of course, our families went to the same church. Around Christmastime, like many others, our church had a Christmas program planned, and they needed a little girl to play a role in the performance. I can still remember the way my heart hurt when I found out they didn't choose me and had chosen my friend for the role. But the hurt I felt was not from them choosing my friend; the hurt was because all I could hear in that moment was that they didn't choose me. True or not, at just five years old, I thought very clearly: *The reason they must not have chosen me is because I'm chubby and not cute like her.* While I don't feel the same pain and hurt today, as a mom to my own little girl now, replaying that memory is still heartbreaking to me.

I can't help but think about my daughter. I never want her to doubt her identity or her value, but because she's human, I know she'll ask that question throughout her life. My prayer now is not that she would never ask the question, but that she will always know Who to ask.

A Little Pro Tip

No matter who you are, how you see yourself, or where you've come from, there's about a 99.99% chance you've asked this question before. Make no mistake, this is a loaded question. Some of us ask ourselves, some of us ask the people around us, some of us ask people we don't even know on social media and, in desperate times, some of us do all the above.

The question "Who am I?" doesn't always sound like those three little words. It comes in all kinds of packages: thoughts, thought patterns, feelings of doubt, and often anxiety. "Who am I?" often looks like comparing gifts, talents, abilities, looks, calling, or story. It can mean comparing your family, how you were raised, or even your perspective of yourself to that of someone else. Whether we realize it or not, we ask the question "Who am I?" many times throughout our lives and in many different seasons. Some of us, when we might be walking through an especially difficult season, even ask ourselves this question multiple times each day. As a culture and a people, I believe we're crying out for the answer to this question more than we ever have before.

So, you might be thinking, *I ask myself this all the time.* I want to begin our journey together by reminding you that asking questions, even this one, is not bad! But asking this question to the wrong person could be detrimental.

I used to believe discovering who we are was something we figured out when we were young, but I realized with every new season, I was redis-covering who I am again and again. Throughout my life, I've watched others far beyond me in years either not know who they are in a season of life or, in some cases, never truly know who they are at all. As women, we go through many seasons that cause us to re-ask the question "Who am I?" Not to mention the pressure of social media and its access to people and women across the world, which has made countless women feel less valuable, less original, less worthy, and less captivating.

> **As women, we go through many seasons that cause us to re-ask the question "Who am I?"**

This three-word question can quickly feel overwhelming and all-consuming when we don't have an answer. In some seasons, many of us become so crippled by the lack of an answer that it completely transforms the way we think, feel, and act.

One of the most life-changing moments for me came from asking God this question at 22 years old. I was living out a dream of being a professional backup dancer, traveling the world, experiencing different places, and making memories. But this dream wasn't as perfect as I imagined it would be. I was incredibly confused and lacked peace, not to mention I was also in a relationship that was causing that confusion. Throughout that season of life and through a relationship that lasted four years, you could definitely say I was asking the right question to the wrong person. And, because I was asking the right question to the wrong person, I remained confused and anxious.

So, I want to give you a little pro-tip, straight from my hard-won reality to your heart! Whether you're 15, 55, or 95 and reading this right now, you will never discover who you truly are by asking more questions about who you are.

Discovering your true identity, your God-given DNA, and your personality — what makes you and shakes you — will only happen by discovering more about the One who made you. Whether you picked up this book believing in God or doubting every part of Him, I can promise you that He is the way to the contentment and peace with yourself that you're searching for.

Our Truest Self and Deepest Purpose

At 22 years old, I decided I was done living in the in-between. I wanted to live in the fullness that Jesus came to give me and died to lavish upon me, so I ended the relationship, quit my dream job, moved to a new city, made new friends, and began believing for God's very best for my life. To that point in my life, those were the hardest decisions I had ever made, but now I can tell you that they led to the best seasons of my life.

Completely starting over caused me to ask the question, "God, who am I?" At least this time, I was asking the right person! I had held on so tightly to the things I was doing and the people I was doing them with that, without them, I truly didn't know who I was.

One day, as I sat in my apartment in Nashville, God reminded me of a video my mom had sent me months earlier. In the video, I was about three years old, standing in the playroom of my home. I grabbed the karaoke mic and said with great confidence, "I love Jesus."

In that moment, God was gently reminding me that the most important title I would ever have is simply being "His," a daughter.

What does a three-year-old have to offer? What important thing can a three-year-old achieve? Not much. And that was the point. He didn't want me to achieve anything, be anything, or do anything *for* Him. He didn't care how much Scripture I had memorized, how many followers I had on social media, how many people approved or disapproved of the relationship I was in, or how successful I was by my or anyone else's standards. God just wanted me to know whose I was — I was His. And when we know we are His, we discover our truest self and our deepest purpose.

God just wanted me to know whose I was — I was His.

Now, let me be clear — I'm not asking you to quit your job, move to a new town, or completely start your life over. But I do want to ask if there's something, anything, holding you back from being who you truly are. I know that can be a bit of an overwhelming question, so it's okay if you don't know right now; we'll come back to this . . .

Although my story involved moving and starting over in many areas of life, I can tell you that it wasn't all about those external changes. The physical changes were a tangible result of letting go and letting Jesus show me who He is and *who I am because of Him.*

You're in a Beautiful Place

Maybe you're in a new season of life, and you feel like you're back at the starting line. Maybe you just moved to college, or maybe your kids just left the house and you're rediscovering life as an empty nester. Maybe you just got married or maybe you're pregnant, and your body is changing like crazy. Maybe you're a grandma now, or maybe life threw you a curveball you didn't see coming, and you don't even know what to call the season you're in. If I could put my hand over your forehead right now, the way my dad always would, and speak *peace* over your mind and *rest* over your heart, that's exactly what I would do.

The truth is, though you may not feel like it now, you're in a beautiful place. You've got a really good Friend ready to walk with you, ready to work with you, ready to show you *who He is and who you are because of Him.* Whether it's for the first time or whether it's for

> **The truth is, though you may not feel like it now, you're in a beautiful place.**

the hundredth time, it's never a bad idea to ask your Father, to ask Jesus, to remind you who you are.

One of my favorite passages of Scripture is found in Song of Solomon 2:10–15 (TPT). This passage was so transformational in my life, and I believe it is what your Father is saying to you right now:

Arise, my dearest. Hurry, my darling. Come away with me! I have come as you have asked to draw you to my heart and lead you out. For now is the time, my beautiful one. The season has changed, the bondage of your barren winter has ended, and the season of hiding is over and gone. The rains have soaked the earth and left it bright with blossoming flowers. The season for singing and pruning the vines has arrived. I hear the cooing of doves in our land, filling the air with songs to awaken you and guide you forth. Can you not discern this new day of destiny breaking forth around you? The early signs of my purposes and plans are bursting forth. The budding vines of new life are now blooming everywhere. The fragrance of their flowers whispers, "There is change in the air." Arise, my love, my beautiful companion, and run with me to the higher place. For now is the time to arise and come away with me. For you are my dove, hidden in the split-open rock. It was I who took you and hid you up high in the secret stairway of the sky. Let me see your radiant face and hear your sweet voice. How beautiful your eyes of worship and lovely your voice in prayer. You must catch the troubling foxes, those sly little foxes that hinder our relationship. For they raid our budding vineyard of love to ruin what I've planted within you. Will you catch them and remove them for me? We will do it together.

I want to point out the very end of the passage to you, where He says, "You will do it all by yourself." Oh wait, He never said that!

He says, "We will do it together." No matter what season you're discovering yourself in, to walk through it effectively, you cannot

He says, "We will do it together."

do it alone. You need your maker, the One who knit you together in your mother's womb and ordained every single one of your days before a single one of them came to be (Psalm 139:16). Simply discovering more about yourself will never do anything for you. But, discovering more of who Jesus is, what He has done for you, and how deeply He loves you will change absolutely everything.

You Are His

In Matthew 16, Jesus asks His disciples, *"Who do you say I am?" Simon Peter answered, "You are the Messiah, the Son of the living God." Jesus replied, "Blessed are you, Simon son of Jonah, for this was not revealed to you by flesh and blood, but my Father who is in heaven. And I tell you that you are Peter, and on this rock I will build my church, and the gates of Hades will not overcome it."* (vv. 15–18, NIV). Peter didn't come up with this revelation on his own. It was revealed to him by God.

You have a Father who walks with you closely, too, who wants to show you who He is all over again — or maybe for the first time — and how much He loves you.

Notice that right after Peter acknowledges Jesus as the Son of the living God, Jesus turns around and speaks identity over Peter, calling him by name and speaking purpose over his life. This is how it works when we see Jesus rightly for who He is and what He came to do in our lives. We begin to see ourselves as Jesus sees us: for who we truly are and what we were made to do.

Throughout our lives, we're given many different titles. We go through seasons of playing many different roles. If you're a college student, you may be associated with a certain sorority, club, or team, but you won't be in those circles forever (although you may feel like you will right now)! The day will come when you graduate or move on to a different season of life, and the things that once kept you busy and gave you a sense of purpose won't be your reality anymore. And, just like the day you left for college, you will step into a new chapter of life with new titles and new roles.

The same transition happens when you get married. You drop the title of being single. You're no longer going out on dates; you're a wife now, with new roles and new responsibilities. But what if you tried to carry your title as a single lady into your marriage? Or what if you started a new job with a new title but still told everyone your old title? This would create dysfunction. We often get our temporary titles and roles so twisted up with who we truly are, but not one of these titles can satisfy the deep longings of our soul, and none of the temporary

The only lasting title, role, or position that we will ever hold is the same one we will take with us when we leave this earth. Simply, being "His."

roles we hold can truly tell us who we really are. The only lasting title, role, or position that we will ever hold is the same one we will take with us when we leave this earth. Simply, being "His."

When you realize *and believe* you're "His," this doesn't just produce temporary, circumstantial confidence; it births within *you* supernatural faith.

You are His. You are a daughter of the only Father whose love is totally and completely perfect. He longs for you to experience the fullness of life found in an identity that is yours for the taking.

Daughter, you are God's chosen treasure — set apart as His devoted one. He called you out of darkness to experience His marvelous light, and now He claims you as His very own. He did this so that you would broadcast His glorious wonders throughout the world. (1 Peter 2:9, TPT)

Chapter Two
Wake Up, Daughter

You are a daughter! If I were having a cup of coffee with you now, I would remind you of this again and again.

Because of the world we live in and the daily distractions that come at us a hundred miles an hour, I know how hard it is to hear and truly receive the depth of these words.

What I feel so deeply and wish I could say to you as a friend, face-to-face, is simply, "It's time to wake up!" Or, like the words of King Solomon that we read in Chapter 1, it's time to "arise." Hurry! Don't wait another minute.

I'll never forget one moment I had with a close friend as she said something very similar to me. I was on a tour bus one evening before going out on stage. At that time, I was still living with a half-broken heart and still learning how to let go of a relationship that was so familiar yet so destructive to me. I was learning to see clearly again, but it was a process, to say the least. Sometimes letting go of things we've found our identity in can require a full-on detox.

On the back of the bus that night, my friends surrounded me and began speaking life over me and praying for me. When they had finished, my friend looked me in the eyes and said, "Lane, it's time to take the blanket off." When she said this, she motioned like she was removing a covering from over my head. I don't know what exactly happened in that moment, but something shifted in my heart and my whole being. My countenance changed, my joy returned, and I suddenly felt like myself again — the me that I hadn't seen or heard from in a really long time.

From an outside perspective at that point, it looked like I was starting over, but in the deepest parts of my being and the depths of my soul, everything felt right once again. Suddenly, I had peace again. Suddenly, I felt like the person I was always meant to be. I had sacrificed peace in my heart for so long out of fear of letting go, fear of being less than, and ultimately, fear of God not coming through on His faithfulness to me.

Though this season was many years ago, it was one of the most pivotal times in my life. It sent me into freedom, into fullness, and into the satisfaction my heart had been longing for.

A Whole New World

This may be exactly where you are right now. Whether it's a relationship, whether it's a friendship, or maybe it has absolutely nothing to do with anyone else but you. Yet, as I'm talking about the lack of peace I was living in and stepping into a world of freedom, something within your heart leapt. Maybe you're seeing a glimmer of hope for yourself. I believe you desire true peace, true joy, and true satisfaction so badly, but something keeps telling you that you can't have these things. Maybe something or someone keeps telling you that you don't deserve them.

I was once in this exact place. I was once deeply confused. I wanted to believe that God had more for my life, but believing that enough to let go of what had become comfortable was incredibly hard. Isn't it strange how we can get so comfortable in something that causes us so much heartache?

A world so beautiful, so easy, so light. A life so free!

But my goodness, there is a whole new world out there just waiting for you. A world so beautiful, so easy, so light. A life so free! A life so fulfilling. A world so much better than the one you've been living in, full of fear, full of doubt, and full of insecurities.

Waking Up . . .

Now, I know a lot of us are not morning people, but I'm not talking about waking up like we do each day. I'm talking about taking the blanket off that is keeping you from the light. I'm talking about your soul, the deepest part of who you are, waking up to the God-given, Jesus-bought, lavishly loved identity that has been imputed to your life.

You might be thinking, *Did she just say imputed?* And the answer is yes. And since I said it, I want to take a nosedive into what this word means for your life.

So many of us, in fact, most of us, go through our days having no idea of the gift that has been lavished upon us. Whether we grew up in church or whether we've never even stepped foot in church, for so many of us, actually all of us, we haven't even scratched the surface of the magnitude of what the Father intended for us.

Psalm 145:3 says, *"Lord, you are great and worthy of the highest praise! For there is no end to the discovery of the greatness that surrounds you"* (TPT). And since there is no end, we have so much to discover!

There's so much to being a daughter, yet somehow it feels like being a daughter has become a cheesy Christian term for a girl who is also a believer in Jesus. But as you read this right now, I really don't want you to miss this because it just might change your life if it hasn't already.

"Imputed" is not a word you hear often, yet it means so much to those who believe in Jesus. If it weren't for what has been imputed to us, we wouldn't have a faith at all, or our faith would be without real hope. Something being imputed is much like giving a gift; yet with a gift, you still have to receive it. But when something is imputed to you, it's like it's automatically, permanently placed in your account without the need for your acceptance. This is what God has done with the spotless righteousness of Jesus for you and me. When you believe in Jesus, the righteousness of Christ that you did absolutely nothing to earn is imputed to you. He has imputed His righteousness to us, yet so many of us still wonder if God really loves us or if we've truly been forgiven.

When you believe in Jesus, the righteousness of Christ that you did absolutely nothing to earn is imputed to you.

Now, I'm not saying that there is no need for us to receive Jesus. What I am saying is that when you receive Jesus, you gain full access to that whole new world I was talking about without doing anything to earn it.

As believers, we often think we know this, yet many of us still live a life based on what we think we've earned or deserve.

In Romans 4:20–22, speaking of Abraham, the Bible says,

"He did not waver at the promise of God through unbelief, but was strengthened in faith, giving glory to God, and being fully convinced that what He had promised He was also able to perform. And therefore, 'it was accounted to him for righteousness'" (NKJV).

Now, here's where it becomes personal to you and me. Romans 4:23–25 says,

"Now it was not written for his sake alone that it was imputed to him, but also for us. It shall be imputed to us who believe in Him who raised up Jesus our Lord from the dead, who was delivered up because of our offenses, and was raised because of our justification" (NKJV).

My daughter is two years old now. When I think about her, it is truly impossible to comprehend how

My daughter is two years old now. When I think about her, it is truly impossible to comprehend how much I love her. much I love her. I don't love her for what she can do for me; I just love her because of *who* she is as my daughter. I'm not sitting around watching her every move to see if she pleases me; I'm forever pleased with her simply because she is mine. Yet somehow, many of us still see God like this. In fact, many of us still believe He is punishing us for our sin.

When Jesus died on the cross, all of our sin, all of our shame, and all of our unrighteousness was imputed to Him. Our sin and our wrongdoing was dealt with once and for all. Our sin was imputed to Him so that His righteousness could be imputed to us. When Jesus breathed His last breath before dying on the cross, He said, *"It is finished"* (John 19:30, NIV). Jesus is not going back to the cross every time you sin because all the punishment that we deserved was already placed upon Him, imputed to Him, and dealt with once and for all.

Seeing Him for Who He Is

I think the reason so many of us feel a lack of identity is because our true identity is at war with our flesh. While your soul may know you have all that you need in Jesus, your mind often tells you to "do better, try harder, prove yourself."

Let's be honest though. If God wanted us to continue trying to prove ourselves, He wouldn't have sent Jesus. God wanted right relationship with you, so He did everything in order for you to have it.

Ephesians 1:5–6 says,

"For it was always in his perfect plan to adopt us as his delightful children, through our union with Jesus, the Anointed One, so that his tremendous love that cascades over us would glorify his grace — for the same love he has for the Beloved, Jesus, he has for us. And this unfolding plan brings him great pleasure!" (TPT).

I don't know where you've come from, and I don't know your story or what all you've walked through. But I do know that it was always part of God's plan to call you His own. I do know He loves you more than you can comprehend. And I do know He looks at you with the eyes of a good Father, with such pure, unconditional, unimaginable love.

When my husband Clayton looks at our daughter Rhonny, it's hard to describe what I see in his eyes. The love of a good father is so deep, so vast, so high. It is protective, affirming, healing, and redeeming. The way that Rhonny trusts Clayton's love for her as a young child is the way we were meant to trust Jesus and draw near in perfect trust to our heavenly Father.

Rhonny is able to trust Clayton so freely because she has no question that her daddy loves her. She doesn't doubt for one moment that she's his daughter.

Oftentimes, the reason we don't see ourselves as daughters of God is because we don't see Him for who He is as a loving, heavenly Father. Though our identity as daughters of God is imputed to us, so many of us don't live in the reality of this because we don't live in the reality of who our good Father

Seeing ourselves as beloved daughters begins by seeing Him as our loving Father.

is. Seeing ourselves as beloved daughters begins by seeing Him as our loving Father.

A Loving Father

Before we dive into this, I just want to stop for a second and acknowledge that you may have never been able to put the words "loving" and "father" into the same sentence. In fact, you might have experienced quite the opposite. Maybe you experienced a mixture, and you've never really felt sure or affirmed in the love of your earthly dad. If that's true, I just want to say I'm so, so sorry.

Although my personal story is different and I grew up knowing the deep, affirming love of an earthly father, I also know I did nothing to earn or deserve that love. My heart breaks for you if you have not personally had the relationship with your dad that every daughter longs for, but I also believe that there is a God, a perfect heavenly Father, who wants to heal, restore, and redeem every ounce of brokenness you've endured. And that is my hope and prayer for you.

If you can't find who you have believed God to be in the person of Jesus, then you have a misunderstanding of God.

So, who is the Father? And how do we know that He is loving?

In John 14:9, Jesus said, *"Whoever has seen me has seen the Father"* (ESV). The way we get to know the Father is by looking at Jesus, because He and the Father are one. If you can't find who you have believed God to be in the person of Jesus, then you have a misunderstanding of God.

There's a beautiful story in John chapter eight that so clearly depicts just how good the Father's heart is for His kids and, more specifically in this case, for His daughters.

One day, Jesus sat down to speak to a crowd that had gathered around Him. Then, in the middle of His teaching, religious people (people who thought they knew it all and who thought they were righteous on their own) busted in, pressed through the crowd, and placed a woman in front of Jesus and everyone else, who had just been caught sleeping around. The religious people wanted Jesus to stone the woman for what she had done. They placed her in the middle of everyone because they wanted her to feel ashamed and embarrassed.

But Jesus doesn't shame the woman. He doesn't jump in on the empty chatter and start discussing everything the woman had ever done wrong. Instead, He turns to her accusers and says, *"He who is without sin among you, let him throw a stone at her first"* (John 8:7, NKJV). One by one, the woman's accusers walked away, leaving only Jesus and the woman standing alone. And, like a good, good father, Jesus turns to the woman and says, *"Neither do I condemn you; go and sin no more"* (v. 11).

This is what a really, really good dad does for his children. The heart of Jesus for the woman is the heart of the good Father for His daughter. I can only imagine the love the woman must have felt that day. What a rollercoaster of emotions she must've had . . . what a range of thoughts! In one moment, she thought she might be stoned, and in another moment, after her sins were on display for everyone, she was set free.

Have you ever experienced how liberating this is? There's something so life-changing, something so powerful, that takes place when we let someone in on the things we're not proud of and they still love us.

Do you know that the woman in this story is actually every single one of us? Jesus knows absolutely everything about us. The good, the bad, the ugly, and even the really ugly, and He still chose us when we were right in the middle of our sin.

Jesus knows absolutely everything about us. The good, the bad, the ugly, and even the really ugly, and He still chose us when we were right in the middle of our sin.

Romans 5:8 says, *"But God demonstrates His own love toward us, in that while we were still sinners, Christ died for us"* (NKJV).

Like the woman caught in the very act of adultery who was defended and loved by Jesus even in the midst of her accusers, your Father stands by your side, ready to defend you, love you, and set you free.

You are His DAUGHTER! The one that He loves and the one that He gave His life for. The one that He defends and the one that He sets free.

Daughter, your loving Father demonstrated His own love toward you, in that while you were still a sinner, Christ died for you. (Romans 5:8, NKJV)

I hope it brings *freedom* to your soul to know that the gospel is the only thing that is too good to be true and is still true!

Chapter 3
Come to the River

Before we go any further, I want to stop and acknowledge that you may be feeling like this is all a bit too good to be true. Maybe thoughts like, *Laney, you don't know what I've been through . . . Laney, you don't know what I've done . . . Laney, that's great and all, but I just don't know if I can believe all of that . . .* are going through your head right now.

Maybe this reality of being His daughter feels too good to be true. But I hope it encourages your heart to know that even after about 25 years of knowing Jesus, it still feels too good to be true to me as well.

I hope it brings freedom to your soul to know that the gospel is the only thing that is too good to be true and is still true! Life with Jesus is an invitation to come to the river — the river of life, the river of peace, the river of living water.

In John 7:37–38, Jesus said,

"If anyone thirsts, let him come to Me and drink. He who believes in Me, as the Scripture has said, out of his heart will flow rivers of living water" (NKJV).

"Anyone" in this passage is referring to you and me. We long, we thirst, and we need the living water that satisfies and quenches the deep desires of our souls. And Jesus is the "living water."

Perplexed But Not in Despair

You might be in a season where you feel like no one sees you. You may feel completely forgotten. You may feel lost, broken, even confused. But what you're feeling now is not what is true about who you are.

Our feelings can tell us a lot, but we must know our feelings don't always tell us the truth. Our feelings can guide us; they can help us uncover what it is we're going through or believing about ourselves, but what they're telling us is not always the truth.

There have been many times in my life where I have "felt" worthless. Many times in my life where I've "felt" unimportant. I've felt broken, I've felt lost, I've felt helpless, hopeless, and confused. And though my feelings have tried to tell me who I am, I've learned that they actually don't have that kind of authority over me.

Second Corinthians 4:8 has become an anthem for my family, a banner we hold high. It says, *"We are hard-pressed on every side, yet not crushed; we are perplexed, but not in despair"* (NKJV).

What a beautiful promise we have in Jesus. This verse holds the hope of heaven and the hope for us as children of God — daughters of light.

Eighteen months after we had Rhonny, my husband and I found out we were pregnant again. A couple months later, we found out we were having a little boy! And one month after that, we found out he no longer had a heartbeat.

The shock, the overwhelming sense of loss, and the depth of heartache is hard to put into words. I had believed God for a son; He gave me a son, and now my son is gone. As I'm sure you can imagine, so many thoughts swarmed my mind. I didn't know how to make sense of all that I was feeling and thinking.

We were surrounded by family and friends. People sent flowers, meals, gifts, and words of encouragement. All these things meant so much to us and reminded us that we weren't alone, but as we walked the journey of healing (and still do), I can tell you that nothing compared to the deep sense and the deep knowing that we have HOPE. And it wasn't something we had to go chase down; no, I felt hope holding us, healing us, and speaking to us.

The hope we had was Jesus.

The hope we had was Jesus. Though I'd never known such deep heartache, I had also never experienced the depth of the Father's comfort that meets us in those moments of what "feels" like despair.

As I searched for words to explain my feelings and emotions to those around us, God led me to this passage in 2 Corinthians 4:8.

Suddenly I felt like I had words to describe what both my motherly heart and my spirit, as a daughter, was feeling. This experience had left me perplexed; it was a moment in my journey with Jesus that I'll never forget and one I still can't theologically explain. I had so many questions, like why this had happened, yet somehow there was a deep knowing in my soul, a deep assurance, that I was not in despair.

I cannot answer all the questions as to "why" my son is not here. I'll be honest and tell you I actually have no idea. My mind is still perplexed as to what happened and why, but I can tell you that though I've cried and longed for him, his absence here does not leave me in despair. I will see my son face to face one day, and oh what a heavenly day (truly) that will be! I cannot wait!

You may be reading this right now, and the things I'm saying are resonating deeply within you. You may have walked through the loss of your own child or the loss of someone you hold so dear, and you feel despair. I'm not here to shame you for your feelings, but I'm here as a friend to usher you back into the hope that is yours as a daughter.

If I could just give you a hug right now, that is what I would love to do and remind you, daughter, though you may "feel" like it, you are not in despair.

There are moments we go through in life that leave us gasping for air. Circumstances that sometimes leave us feeling hopeless and helpless. I want to remind you that, though your circumstances and your feelings may try to tell you that you're hopeless and helpless, as a daughter, you are never hopeless or helpless.

> ... when you belong to Jesus, no one can tell you who and what you are but Him!

Your feelings do not tell you who you are, your circumstances do not tell you who God is, and when you belong to Jesus, no one can tell you who and what you are but Him!

Plans to Prosper You

If you've spent any time in church, you probably learned Jeremiah 29:11 in Sunday school. It reads, *"For I know the plans I have for you," says the* LORD, *"plans to prosper you not to harm you, plans to give you hope and a future"* (NIV).

What a promise this is to us as His children! So deep, so true, yet there is more to this verse than many of us have ever been told in Sunday school. This verse was originally translated from the Hebrew language, as was the entire Old Testament of the Bible.

I want to dive into what some of these words meant in their original language. I like to keep things simple and to the point, so I'm going to do my best to make this short, sweet, and easy to understand!

First, let's look at *"For I know."* The word "know" here, was originally translated from the word *Yada* (יָדַע), in Hebrew. As do many of our English words, the word *yada* in Hebrew takes on many different meanings, and though the word *yada* still means to "know," I want you to know the meaning is more vast than our English translation of the word. This word isn't like how we say, "Yada yada yada" when something is unimportant to us, because *yada* actually has great importance to us as children of God, as it is used in the Bible.

"Yada" is used in the Bible nearly 1000 times, for a variation of meanings, but today I want to highlight to you that the word **"yada"** has a covenant meaning. Often times the word we read as "Chosen" in the Bible, was translated from the Hebrew word "yada." *Yada* is also used to describe God's complete knowledge of creation — absolutely nothing can be hidden from Him.

How amazing it is that at the same time He is declaring the depth of His knowledge of us, He simultaneously is declaring His forever covenant with us.

As people, oftentimes we wait till we know all the details before we commit to something.

We want to know what's behind the curtain before we say, "I do." But Jesus said, "I do," to you way before you ever said, "I do," to Him. He said, "I do love you." "I do see you." And oh how "I do know you, and I've chosen you."

What is so amazing about the love of Jesus is that He committed His love to us long before we ever knew Him, chose Him, or would have been considered worth choosing.

Next, let's look at the word "plans" in *"the plans I have for you."* Oftentimes when we hear this verse, we think of it as if every day of our lives is written on a concrete tablet, but you might find it interesting to know that's not what it means exactly. The original word in Hebrew that has been translated into "plans" was *"machashavah"* (מַחֲשָׁבָה) (I dare you to try to say that out loud).

There are several different meanings to the word *machashavah*. In Jeremiah 29:11, we often see this word either translated into the word "plans" or "thoughts," but this Hebrew word also means to invent, plot, or design, [1] implying that God is always creating something new for us.

The plans God has for you, He is continually making for your good. It's easy to think that once we mess up, we have messed up God's total plan for our lives, and now we will live with second best or even third best every time we mess

> **The plans God has for you, He is continually making for your good.**

up. But since God is always working on our behalf, inventing, plotting, and designing new plans for us, messing up His plan for our lives is impossible.

We definitely won't skip over the next part! *"Plans to prosper you . . ."* The word prosper here is the Hebrew word *shalom* (שָׁלוֹם). You might be familiar with this Hebrew word, yet still many of us don't know the depth of its meaning for us as children of God. This Hebrew word *shalom* is also referenced to mean peace, harmony, wholeness, completeness, prosperity, and health. [2] Wow! Did you know that these are the kinds of plans God has for you? Plans for you to live in His peace, in harmony with His spirit within you, restored, made whole, and complete — lacking nothing, prospering in your soul and in your health.

"Not to harm you . . ." Sometimes, as believers, I think we skip over this part a little too quickly as well. In multiple translations, this has been translated into *"not of evil."* The word "evil" has been translated from the Hebrew word *ra* (רַע), meaning that which is evil, wicked, trouble, affliction, harm, and adversity. [3]

Take a look at the biblical meaning of *ra* (evil) one more time. Have you ever wondered if God "caused" any of these things in your life? I can definitely say that I've walked through some "evil" things before and wondered if God caused them, but I hope this brings some peace to your soul to know that the evil you have experienced was not from your loving heavenly Father. The evil we experience in this world is from the evil one, the enemy of our souls and the enemy of our true identity.

> . . . know that the evil you have experienced was not from your loving heavenly Father.

"Plans to give you hope and a future . . ." The word "future" here was originally translated from the Hebrew word *Acharit* (אַחֲרִית). Something so interesting is that the root word of *Acharit* is *Achar*, which has the meaning of past and behind. [4] I believe this is because our heavenly Father, the God of the universe, is outside time and space. The God who makes new plans for your future also makes new plans to fill your past with hope.

Psalm 139:5 says, *"You've gone into my future to prepare the way, and in kindness you follow behind me to spare me from the harm of my past. You have laid your hand on me"* (TPT).

Have you ever walked through a season full of ups and downs? Some decisions maybe you wish you wouldn't have made, or something happened to you that seemed really bad, yet you look back later and see that what seemed like evil in your life, now looked like something for your good? I know I have, and every time, it amazes me just as much. Every time, it's beyond what I could've imagined or seen as possible, yet God does what only He can do.

> **. . . I wait with expectation to see how He steps into what is now our past to fill it with hope and how He redeems what is our future.**

I can't yet see every way God will restore hope to Clayton and me with what we walked through with our little boy. I do not believe that God caused evil in my life or caused evil for my family. But I wait with expectation to see how He steps into what is now our past to fill it with hope and how He redeems what is our future.

He's Inviting You

No matter where you are today, the invitation to come to the river is always available to you. The river is peace, harmony, wholeness, completeness, prosperity, and health. The river is life to your soul and peace to your mind. The river will redeem every single thing that the enemy meant for harm. The river is faithful.

Jesus is the river, and we just get to come.

Daughter, He knows the plans He has for you.
Plans to prosper you and not to harm you.
Plans to give hope to your future and to your past.
(Jeremiah 29:11)

Take your shoes off.
Feel the *new* ground.
You have no shoes
to fill.

Chapter 4
Take Your Shoes Off

Take your shoes off. Feel the new ground. You have no shoes to fill.

I want to liberate you today with the same words that Jesus used to liberate me years ago. I was in a church conference with about four thousand other people. In a moment of worship, so gently, I heard the Holy Spirit say to me, "Laney, take your shoes off, feel the new ground, you have no shoes to fill."

In that moment, I knew God wasn't actually talking about the shoes on my feet, He was speaking to the pressure I had been putting on myself to be something I'm not.

No matter what our current roles are in life, we often feel the need to "fill the shoes." Many of us wake up to demands, pressures, timelines, and people who count on us. The weight of expectation that we feel can get heavy, hard to bear, and in the end, unsustainable. When we feel tired and worn out, we feel the need to perform, to make it work, and to "fill the shoes."

One of the many beautiful things about belonging to Jesus, about being a "daughter" and being called His very own, is that when you said "I do" to Him, you said goodbye to the need to strive and perform. You no longer have to be or pretend to be something that you're not because who you are is enough, simply because HE is enough.

Now, I'll be transparent with you, as I would if you were sitting on my couch, and I'll let you know that I'm preaching to my own choir! Although I know this is what is true about who I am and what has been given to me, living from this truth is not always my first instinct. Retraining your mind takes time, and I'll be the first to admit that I'm

Retraining your mind takes time, and I'll be the first to admit that I'm still learning and Jesus is still rewiring some things in there.

still learning and Jesus is still rewiring some things in there.

Personally, my roles in life are wife, mom, daughter, sister, and friend. In this current season and during most hours of the day, I play wife and mom. Sometimes being a mom is hard. If you're a mom, you might be shouting, "Say it again!" Although being a mom is truly the most amazing and life-giving thing in the world, it can also feel like the most exhausting thing in the world.

There are days when I feel defeated. There are days when I feel like I have no clue what I'm doing. There are days when I get frustrated. There are days when I'm really, really tired. And when these moments come, within my soul, it feels like there's a choice to make. Will I let go? Or will I muster up the strength and keep going?

Now if I posted those options on social media, unfortunately, one would get a lot more praise (or "likes"). As people, we tend to gravitate toward stories where people push through, buck up, and be strong. But what if I told you that Jesus actually doesn't desire for you to buck up and press on? What if I told you that, out of these two options, Jesus would choose "letting go" for you?

The world we live in is run by so many systems. And because we weren't truly made for systems, it's easy to start feeling the pressure to perform. To be what everyone wants you to be, expects you to be, and hopes you will be. To look good, feel good, and smell good all the time. We walk into rooms full of people — friends, or strangers — and feel the need to pretend like we didn't just completely fall apart in the car. We feel the need to hide that on the inside because we actually don't feel as secure as we may look on the outside.

Made Whole . . .

My husband, Clayton, is the most amazing man that I know. Although I once said that I would never marry anyone younger than me, I stand corrected, as he is two years and ten months younger than I am. When I met him, I was living in an apartment with friends, and he was still in college, living on campus. I spent my college years traveling as a backup dancer, so dating him in that season was the extent of my college experience.

Although on paper it might look like we grew up very similarly, as we got to know each other, we learned how differently our growing up was . . .

On our second date, I remember asking Clayton, "So what do you believe?" And he said to me, "I just follow Jesus." He didn't even know the weight of what he was saying in that moment, but his words were a breath of fresh air for me. I was ready to say "I do" right then and there! There was something so refreshing to me about the simplicity of his answer. I often remember his words as a reminder to myself and for my family that following Jesus is always more than enough — and often a whole lot more simple than we make it.

I was ready to say "I do" right then and there!

What I didn't know is that those words came out of Clayton's mouth before he even knew the full truth of them.

What I didn't know at the time is that Clayton grew up believing performance was part of earning

God's grace. As a child, there were times Clayton went to church conventions and competitions where he was given a score from judges based on how well he gave a sermon or led a worship song. Certain kids were given trophies based on their scores, while others received nothing.

So often, I think too many of us still see our faith journey like this. If we do good, then we deserve what is good, but if we do bad, we deserve what is bad.

Many of us still believe that we get what we deserve. But if this is true, what did Jesus die for?

Many of us still believe that we get what we deserve. But if this is true, what did Jesus die for? If our faith is built on our performance, then Jesus died in vain.

As Clayton and I continued dating, I got to see firsthand the rewiring God was doing in his heart and mind — the crossing over from performance-based religion to a simple relationship with Jesus. There was never any doubt in Clayton's mind that God loved him, yet subconsciously, there was a part of himself that he thought

God wouldn't love — his imperfections, weaknesses, and failures.

So many of us, consciously or subconsciously, still see our heavenly Father like this. When we're doing "good" in life, we believe He is close and He must really love us, but in our dark hours, insecurities, and failures, we think He must be far away and He can't even look at us.

But this is so far from the truth. Because of Jesus, God is looking at you with such radiant joy, deep compassion, and love in His heart.

Because of Jesus, God is looking at you with such radiant joy, deep compassion, and love in His heart.

We must remember that Jesus perfectly revealed the Father's heart for us. And He didn't come when we were perfect, but the Bible tells us that Jesus chose to die for us "while we were still sinners" (Romans 5:8). That means that even in your darkest hours, even in the moments you wish to never remember again, that is when He chose you and poured Himself out for you.

The good news about Jesus is that the life He offers isn't for perfect people, but for broken people to be made whole.

You Can Smile

When Clayton and I were engaged and a few months away from getting married, he would come straight to my house every day after work. One day when he got to my house, I could tell something was troubling him. Clayton's countenance was typically light, but on this day I could feel his heaviness. I started asking questions as I typically do, trying to get to the bottom of what was up. Each time I asked, he would say, "I'm fine," yet I could see on his face that everything was not fine.

Something I've learned about my husband since we've been married is that prying doesn't work on him; I have to give him time. That day, I remember feeling a gentle nudge in my spirit to stop prying and give him time. As we sat on the couch, instead, I began just speaking over him what was true. "I love you. I'm so proud of who you are. You're an amazing man. You've been made new. God has you. There is nothing to fear."

I remember tears started rolling down his face, and he immediately began to tell me what was on his mind. He thought I was going to be disappointed with him, that I wouldn't see him the same because, in his eyes, he had really messed up. Yet in that moment, all I could see and sense was how loved he was and how God was looking at him with such pride and awe.

As tears continued to stream down his face, he looked at me like, "Well, now that you know what's wrong, what do you have to say to me?" And without a second thought, the words that came to my heart and out of my mouth were, "Clayton, you can smile. Right now, you don't have to wait another moment."

So often when we fail, we feel like we have to hide . . .

So often when we fail, we feel like we have to hide, and we often feel like we need to sit and think about what we've done, yet God never asked us to do that. Instead, He tells us to remember what HE has done.

In that moment, the reason I was able to tell Clayton he could smile had absolutely nothing to do with Clayton. The reason He could smile in the midst of his shame was because of the righteousness that had been imputed to him when he received Jesus.

Our flesh likes performance-based religion because our flesh likes to feel in control.

Living in this gift of righteousness feels unnatural at first. Our flesh likes performance-based religion because our flesh likes to feel in control. As humans, it is our nature to want to be in control of our plans, our future, our family, and even our own righteousness. Many of us like to feel like we're "good" at being a Christian. Oftentimes we subconsciously think we got something good out of life because we performed well, yet this is the opposite of the gospel.

God's gift to you was that while you were still "bad," while you still didn't measure up, while you still fell short, Jesus, being perfect, made you right with Him. He made you whole. He made you pure, lovely, and forever pleasing to Him (Romans 5:8).

So I want to ask you: what have you been carrying? Where do you feel like you've been striving to earn His love for you? What thing has the enemy made you believe that you must hide? Where do you feel pressure to "perform"?

The invitation for you today, daughter, is to "let go." Stop trying to be what you think everyone expects you to be and fall into His perfection, His righteousness, His strength, and His supply. You can smile, even in the midst of what you've been going through, because God is smiling at you.

Ephesians 1:3 says,

"Every spiritual blessing in the heavenly realm has already been lavished upon us as a love gift from our wonderful heavenly Father, the Father of our Lord Jesus — all because he sees us wrapped into Christ. This is why we celebrate him with all our hearts!" (TPT).

Daughter, you have been wrapped in your wonderful Savior. When He was sought out, captured by His enemies, and led to His accusers, He took your place. When He was wrongly accused, beaten, and led to His crucifixion, He took your place. When He was spat upon, hung on a cross, and tormented by those who killed Him, He took your place.

To live a life based on your performance would be to completely diminish the gospel and the richness of its gift of righteousness.

For you, daughter, He said, *"It is finished!"* (John 19:30, NKJV).

To live a life based on your performance would be to completely diminish the gospel and the richness of its gift of righteousness.

Daughter, take your shoes off.
Feel the new ground that He has put beneath
your feet. You have no shoes to fill.

Chapter 5
Comparing Rightly

You set your alarm for 6 a.m. When 6 a.m comes around, your alarm goes off, and you make it out of bed by 6:30. You planned to have some time to yourself before your kids wake up, before you leave for work, or before you head off to school. You planned to work out, read your Bible, have some time to think and pray. You get up, make the coffee, and suddenly you hear your toddler up an hour before she usually wakes up.

Your workout app won't let you log in, and work decides to call you in an hour early. Suddenly, what seems like a refreshing morning turns into extra work, frustration, and disappointment. You feel like you failed because nothing you intended to do got done. Your new year's resolution is so far gone that you can't even fully remember what it was at this point. And now you feel like a failure, behind, and disappointed with yourself.

At lunchtime, you find yourself scrolling through social media. You see that everyone else in your feed had the time that you hoped for this morning — time to read, time to pray, time to make breakfast, work out, and even make a highlight reel to post about it. You feel something beginning to rise in your chest; something is suddenly troubling you and burdening your heart, but it feels too soon to pinpoint what it is. You go through the rest of your day feeling defeated, discouraged, less than, and honestly a little jealous of everyone else.

A Place of Plenty

This is how the enemy lies to you. It's not often written on the walls. Typically, little by little, one small thing after another builds up until we feel really, really lost and confused about who we are and why we're here.

Do you resonate with this at all? Do you ever just *feel* down? Maybe you feel like you're in a funk, but you're not sure "what" is wrong.

I think this series of unfortunate events, or something like it, is often how this happens. We set goals, we have hopes and expectations, and then when things don't go as we planned, we just feel "blah."

Blah, meaning bland, nothing special, unqualified, discouraged, defeated, and empty. Blah, meaning not full of joy, peace, hope, and satisfaction. Blah, meaning existing, but without the awareness of the goodness of Jesus and the fruit of His Spirit in your life.

Comparison often plays a part in leading us to this place of feeling blah, yet comparison only has power when we don't know what's already been given to us.

When you don't know what you have, it's like comparing what everyone else has to absolutely nothing. But when you know what you've been given as

When you know what you've been given as a daughter, comparison loses its power over you.

a daughter, comparison loses its power over you, because you're no longer comparing from a place of lack but from a place of plenty!

Now you might be thinking, *Laney, are you promising me another hour every morning?* And although I wish I could promise us both that, that isn't what I'm saying! What I'm saying is that being a daughter comes with an inheritance. Being a daughter isn't just a position, it's a right to all that is yours because of Jesus.

Your Inheritance ...

Do you know that all that the Father has is yours?

The story of the prodigal son in Luke 15 is a popular story among people who go to church. If you already know this story, you know the narrative of the son who leaves and comes back is what gets most of the attention, hence why the story is called "the prodigal son," but today I want to draw your attention to the older brother, the brother who stayed home and stayed close to his father.

In this story, there's a father and two sons. One day, the younger son came to his father and said to him, *"Father, give me my share of the estate"* (v. 12, NIV). So the father gave him what was his inheritance, and the son quickly left his father's house and squandered his wealth in wild living. The older brother stayed home. He stayed close; he served and worked in the fields of his father's house, yet something in him was still unsatisfied.

When the younger son came to his senses and realized what he had done, he decided to return home. When the father saw his son coming home from a long way off, he ran to him, kissing him and adorning him with a beautiful robe, a welcome home party, and incredible food. Yet, while all this was happening, the older son was still out working in the field. As the older son came near the house, he could hear the music, the laughter, and the sound of people celebrating his younger brother, who had just wasted everything, and it didn't make sense to him why his younger brother should be celebrated.

In his frustration and hurt, the older brother went to his father and said, "Look, all these years I have been slaving away for you and never disobeyed you, yet you've never thrown a party for me and my friends. How can my brother waste everything you've given him on prostitutes and wild living and you decide to throw him a party?"

But the father replied to his son by saying, "My son, you are always with me, and everything I have is yours."

From an outside perspective, it could seem like only the younger son had wasted everything, yet in reality, the older son had been wasting his inheritance the entire time and had no idea. And this is why I think so many of us can deeply relate to the older son.

Comparison wouldn't be so detrimental to our hearts and our minds if we were comparing rightly. Looking at the goodness and faithfulness of God in someone else's life should not cause us to doubt His goodness and faithfulness in our own lives. Yet, the reason comparison becomes

> **Looking at the goodness and faithfulness of God in someone else's life should not cause us to doubt His goodness and faithfulness in our own lives.**

defeating and life-sucking is because we don't realize that all the Father has is ours.

The older son stayed close, yet he didn't enjoy everything that was already his. He missed out on the celebration because he doubted his father's heart specifically for him. He worked hard, striving to please his father, when his father was already well pleased with him and had given him everything. He was living with his inheritance but not living from it.

> **He was living with his inheritance but not living from it.**

So let's talk about your inheritance.

Daughter, the inheritance that is yours is not one you have to strive for, earn, or achieve. Your heavenly Father is forever pleased with you because He is forever pleased with His Son, Jesus. This inheritance breaks the power of sin and shame over your life. This inheritance is perfect love, so you will never have to live in fear or believe you lack any good thing. This inheritance cannot be taken away from you.

Though I was a backup dancer for several years, I honestly never fully enjoyed my position because

I never fully believed I deserved to be there. There were a lot of things that played into this belief: how I got the job, my lack of technical training, the thousands of other dancers who were more qualified than me, and the voices that were speaking into my life at the time. There were many times where I knew I was being made fun of or that someone was doubting my ability compared to someone else. I was living out a dream, yet within my heart I felt defeated and a great sense of lack. And because I never believed I deserved to be there, I lived fearful of losing my position.

One day, as I was talking to my mom about the fear I felt over losing my job, she said to me, "Laney, you cannot strive to keep something that you did not earn in the first place." Talk about a drop the mic moment! In one moment, years of fear and torment lost their power over me as I realized what my mom was saying was true for absolutely every area of my life.

> "... you cannot strive to keep something that you did not earn in the first place."

Our inheritance is *inherited.* The goodness of God in our lives is simply passed on to us by His extravagant love and mercy. There's nothing in this life that we could ever do to earn or deserve the extent of which God has loved us. That whole time, I wasn't enjoying what I had been given because I was looking for a means to deserve it. I was completely missing the gift that God had given me because I felt like I needed to prove that I earned it. But the truth is, thank God, we don't always get what we deserve in this life! Thank you, Jesus, that the blessings You pour out are not based on our performance but because of Your performance on the cross.

Jesus took what we deserved so that we could live in the abundance of what He deserves. And the greatest blessing He has and will ever give to us is Himself. Many times, we go searching

Jesus took what we deserved so that we could live in the abundance of what He deserves.

for something else because we simply can't see what we've already been given, but God gave us everything our hearts truly long for in Jesus. Though life with

Jesus doesn't mean life without hills and valleys, life with Jesus does promise us Himself in the midst. And it is time for you to know your inheritance and enjoy your inheritance.

When you received Jesus, you inherited the gift of His Holy Spirit. And with the Holy Spirit, you inherited the fruit of His Spirit. In this is love, joy, peace, patience, kindness, goodness, faithfulness, gentleness, and self-control. What more could we truly need in life if we're living from an abundance of these things? When comparison begins to steal from our lives, this is not from a lack of abundance but often a lack of an awareness of this abundance.

Holding Nothing Back

I love the story of Mary and Martha when Jesus comes to visit their home. In the story, Martha is worried and troubled by many things. She is busy in the kitchen, striving and trying to prepare everything for Jesus, while her sister Mary is simply sitting at His feet, hanging on His every word.

In her stress, Martha turned to Jesus and said, *"Lord, don't you care that my sister has left me to do the work by myself? Tell her to help me!"* (Luke 10:40, NIV). But Jesus didn't turn to Mary and tell her to get up from her position of receiving from Him, instead He told Martha, *"Martha, Martha . . . you are worried and upset about many things, but few things are needed — or indeed only one. Mary has chosen what is better, and it will not be taken away from her"* (vv. 41–42, NIV).

I want you to notice that Mary and Martha shared a house. Jesus didn't only come to Mary's house; He showed up in Martha's house too. Yet still, Martha was worried, anxious, and comparing from a sense of lack. Martha had everything Mary had in that moment, yet still she was comparing from a sense of lack. She didn't realize the abundance that was literally in her living room!

And oftentimes, this is us. We don't realize the abundance, the fullness, the gift of Jesus that is in our personal living room. Psalm 34:10 says, *"The lions may grow weak and hungry, but those who seek the LORD lack no good thing"* (NIV).

Before you start comparing, remind yourself of this: "I lack no good thing." All that the Father has, He has freely given to you, holding nothing back.

Daughter, because of Jesus, you have an inheritance that is imperishable, undefiled, and unfading, kept in heaven for you. (1 Peter 1:4)

Chapter 6
The Waiting

There is a moment, when we close the door or turn the light out, that only we and God know what it is we're truly longing and waiting for. Although we often don't share the depths of our desires with everyone, we are all desiring something in just about every season of life. And longing, no matter for what, feels long. Waiting isn't easy, because when you're waiting, that means there's at least a part of your heart that believes you're expecting something to come.

One of the longest seasons of waiting I can remember was the years leading up to when I met my husband. If you're in this season currently, or if you were there many years ago, I think many of us can relate to this season feeling like forever! Whether it was two months or fifteen years, looking toward something without evidence of its fulfillment makes the days slow and the years feel long.

Being married was a deep desire of my heart, something I prayed for often and believed would one day come to be, yet there were many days I remember asking God, "Where is he?" When you're single, it can be hard to stay hopeful when it feels like everyone around you is either dating, engaged, or married. I remember when I broke up with my boyfriend of four years; that very same year, many people I was close to got engaged and married. There were moments where I questioned if I had done the right thing, simply because I longed so deeply to be married and there was no sign of that coming anytime soon.

There are many moments during waiting seasons when other people get what you're hoping for. Sometimes I wish I could say that wasn't the case and absolutely everything in life is fair, but the truth is, it's just not. God didn't want robots;

Life looks differently for every single person, and every one of us has a different story to tell.

He made sons and daughters with free will, free to make our own choices. Life looks differently for every single person, and every one of us has a different story to tell. Yet if you hold on, I promise all of our stories have the same ending, and that is with His faithfulness.

Even in the waiting that is long and sometimes even painful, He is still who He said He is, faithful in all of His ways.

I also sometimes wish I could tell you that you only go through one waiting season in your life, but unfortunately, we go through many waiting seasons, and I've personally found myself in one once again.

Longing for Something You Lost . . .

God brought the most amazing man into my life, and I love him more than I could've ever imagined. Five months into marriage, God was faithful to another deep desire in my heart, and I became a momma — pregnant with our first baby. Rhonny Grace is truly a dream; I could've never fathomed a gift like her. And then we got pregnant with our little boy, Rory,

16 months later. After carrying him for 17 weeks, he went to be with Jesus. And I've never longed for a baby like I do now. This deep longing that I feel is a kind of longing I've never experienced before, because I don't long for something I've never known; I now long for something that I once had.

Before I met Clayton, I didn't know what it was to love someone so deeply. Before we got married, I didn't know what it was for someone to know me fully and completely love me. Before I had Rhonny, I didn't know what it was to have a child and love someone with that kind of love. But when I lost Rory, I knew what it was to love him, and now I know what it is to not spend a life with him. Although I don't believe getting pregnant again will be what completes the healing of my heart, there is a deeper longing to be pregnant now than ever before because I know what a treasure I had been given in my son because of the treasure I have known in my daughter.

So here I am, in the waiting season again, and though the longing feels deeper than it ever has before, I'm grateful for all the other seasons of waiting and longing that have led me to this one. Because again, although the days can feel slow and the year feels long, I've seen enough to know that my God is so much more faithful than I can fathom.

I've seen enough to know that my God is so much more faithful than I can fathom.

There are hard days. There are days that it's hard to look my pregnant best friend in the eyes without crying because I thought we'd be pregnant together. But in those moments, I choose to believe that even in the waiting, I can live like I've already received the promise. And that is a gift that you and I have in common as ones who belong to Jesus.

For What Is Seen Is Temporary, but What Is Unseen Is Eternal

Hebrews 11 is one of my favorite chapters in the Bible of all time. This chapter is all about faith and the heroes of faith in the Old Testament. The chapter starts by saying, *"Now faith is confidence in what we hope for and assurance about what we do not see"* (v. 1, NIV). I want to pause for a second and just say if you're waiting for something right now that you cannot see coming at all, hold on to this promise and hold on to faith. This gift of faith is your secret weapon in even the most painful seasons of waiting. In the moments where what you're waiting for feels impossible, hold on to faith's promise. Faith will carry you and give you a strength that you could never have on your own, because you're not putting your faith in yourself, but your faith is in the One who created the world and everything in it.

Hebrews 11:3 says, *"By faith we understand that the universe was formed at God's command, so that what is seen was not made out of what was visible"* (NIV).

When we're longing for something, it's easy to want to search for the evidence of its arrival. As people, we want to be able to see it with our eyes. But if I could encourage you with what I've learned in my life thus far, don't look for your evidence in what you can see, but look for it in what you cannot — look for your evidence in what is unseen, for what is seen is temporary, but what is unseen is eternal (2 Corinthians 4:18).

As people, we want to be able to see it with our eyes.

When I was 18 years old, I remember asking God what He had for my life. In many ways, at that time, I was looking for a big lit-up sign that said, "Laney, I want you to _____ (fill in the blank) with your life." I thought it would be written in my journal or I thought I would hear a clear word that let me know what I would do for the rest of my days. In some ways, He did that, but not in any way that I thought He would.

One night, after having a conversation about life with my parents, I remember going up to my room and just saying, "God, will You just give me one word? One word to direct me, one word to guide me, one word to show me what to do?" In that moment, I remember simply hearing the word "serve." I remember thinking "Serve, okay, I can do that." Looking back now, I can honestly say that if God had shown me then some of the things that He would eventually lead me into, I would have said, "No way." I would've heard what He asked me to do, looked at what is seen, and said, "That's impossible." But God is so gracious and so kind in how He leads us to have faith in who He is. We do not walk our faith journey alone, but we walk within His Holy Spirit, leading and guiding us the whole way, giving us what we need at just the right time.

After this moment, I remember seeking out a nanny job to serve a family the best I knew how, and I got a job at Chick-fil-A serving chicken. I can still remember my drives to Chick-fil-A and those cute uniform black pants and kitchen shoes. I remember my drives so well because I remember being so honest with God on the way there, telling Him that I hoped to be doing things that were in my heart, like sharing my love for music and dance as a way of ministry. That season, although it only lasted a few months, felt incredibly long because, like I said, "longing is long." As I drove to work, I remember thinking, *God, this isn't exactly what I had in mind.* All my friends were off to college and enjoying new experiences, and I felt like I was back home doing something seemingly insignificant.

What many people didn't know is that while I was working at Chick-fil-A, I was taking more dance classes than I ever had in my life. I was learning full 45-minute sets of choreography, to a show on

YouTube, that I very likely would never perform. I was driving to work at Chick-fil-A, but deep in my heart, I believed God. I believed the things He had put in there were for a purpose. And though currently it looked nothing like I thought or hoped, something in me knew

> ... deep in my heart, I believed God. I believed the things He had put in there were for a purpose.

He was faithful, and I would not be disappointed.

Only three months into working at Chick-fil-A, I got a call from someone who would become a dear friend, Britt Nicole. Britt, who was touring as a Christian music artist, told me one of the dancers in her show couldn't make it and asked me to step in. It just so happened that I already knew all the choreography. What I thought was a one-time opportunity turned into hundreds of shows over four years, the fulfillment of a dream I had in my heart for what felt like a long time. Through one moment with one simple word, God has brought an abundance of direction and fruitfulness in my life. Though there was a season where the waiting felt like forever and the dream seemed impossible, I have seen over and over again that with God, all things are possible. And while we wait, we can wait like we have already received the promise.

Judge Him Faithful Who Has Promised

The fulfillment of the promise may not look like what you thought. Many people in Jesus' day did not believe that He was their savior because He came as a child and a humble servant instead of what a mighty king in that time looked like. They held on too tightly to what they could see instead of what they could not. They wanted signs and wonders instead of realizing the real sign and wonder was Jesus Himself. Jesus was who they had been waiting for, yet many of those who claimed to be waiting for Him were the same ones who crucified Him.

The beautiful promise and fullness of our salvation is found when we look to Jesus. Hebrews 12:2 tells us that He alone is the author and finisher of our faith. So when we wait, we do not wait like even the heroes of faith did in Hebrews 11, looking forward to a promise fulfilled, but we wait within the fulfillment of the promise, which is Jesus Himself.

It's common sense to not live like you have something until you actually do. If you tried to go buy a house right now, but you didn't have any money in your account, then the people selling the house to you would not let you buy the house. You wouldn't move into the house if you didn't pay for it. This is common sense. But there is a whole other realm in the kingdom of God that is eternal, and that is our true reality as believers in Jesus. That is not common sense. Our faith is not in common sense, but our faith is the firm belief in a heavenly realm where we have been seated in Christ Jesus (Ephesians 2:6).

Our faith is not in common sense, but our faith is the firm belief in a heavenly realm where we have been seated in Christ Jesus (Ephesians 2:6).

When God began putting it on my heart to move to a new city, I read Hebrews 11 a lot. Over and over, I read about Abraham and how he went out not knowing where he was going but to receive an inheritance God had promised. In that season, I desperately needed to be reminded that it was okay that I didn't know exactly where I was going, as long as I knew who was going with me and that He was faithful.

Hebrews 11:11 says, *"By faith Sarah herself also received strength to conceive seed, and she bore a child when she was past the age, because she judged Him faithful who had promised"* (NKJV).

> **One of the greatest gifts you have as a daughter is the ability to judge Him faithful who has promised.**

One of the greatest gifts you have as a daughter is the ability to judge Him faithful who has promised. His faithfulness is not up for debate. His faithfulness is not fragile. His faithfulness has been fulfilled in your life, and now you get to live from that promise.

Every time I'm in a new season of waiting, I think about a story of my Aunt Robin, who is my mom's younger sister. When she was a little girl, she had a lump on her lip. They didn't know exactly what it was, but every day, my aunt would speak to it, telling it to fall off in the name of Jesus. My grandparents would find her in her room, practicing how she was going to tell people how God healed her. One day, the lump fell off her lip and into her hand. What I love about this is my aunt didn't wait till she had received her healing to start living like she already had received it. She declared her testimony of what God had done before there was tangible evidence that it had happened.

Now when I'm in a season of waiting or longing, I find myself practicing how I'm going to tell people what He has done. I rehearse in my heart, in my mind, and out of my mouth the story I will tell of His faithfulness. Because I know I'm a daughter, and His faithfulness is mine. I do not live by what is seen, but I live by what is eternal.

Because I know I'm a daughter, and His faithfulness is mine.

When we lost our son, many people would probably look at what we walked through with common sense and question if God was faithful in this season. But though I can't answer all the questions about what happened, I've learned enough to know that I don't live by common sense, but I live by every word He has spoken. I've learned that my circumstances and my partial understanding of this life cannot tell me who God is more than God has told me who He is. For I know that in this life we only see in part, but one day we will see clearly, face to face, and know just as we are fully known (1 Corinthians 13:12).

Daughter, wherever you find yourself today, I want to encourage you, like Sarah, like Abraham, like my Aunt Robin, to judge Him faithful who has promised. Though you may not see it yet, you can already begin to tell of His faithfulness.

Chapter 7

You're Beautiful

"Jesus, You're so beautiful." I've caught myself saying these words many times lately, and then after they've spilled out, I've asked myself, *What does that mean?* These words have uttered out of my mouth and from my heart, yet in my mind I haven't fully understood what it is I'm trying to say. I have been captivated by the beauty of Jesus in this season, yet I can't physically see Him, so how could it be? When we think about beauty, our minds and our eyes often go to what we can see that is beautiful, but I have found that I am most captivated by the beauty in which I can't see. The things that I haven't just seen with my eyes, but the moments that have truly touched my heart.

Most married women will say the day they felt the most beautiful was on their wedding day. You could say it's possibly from the dress, the hair, the makeup, the shoes . . . all the things that often go with getting married. But I'm convinced that none of these things can truly make a woman feel beautiful. The reason most women feel beautiful on their wedding day is because they feel loved!

Some of the moments in my life where I may have looked my best were moments I didn't feel the least bit beautiful. I can still remember sitting in an airport waiting for our plane to arrive when the guy I was dating at the time saw another woman walk by — who was very fit, might I add — and said, "Did you see her? You could look like that." As you can imagine, in that moment, I was crushed. I had a hard enough time comparing myself to other people on my own, but now I was being compared to another woman by the person who told me they loved me.

God has carried me a long way from that moment until now, and my husband has been a huge part of God redeeming my once very confused idea of what is truly beautiful. When Clayton and I were dating, I started to notice that the days I tried really hard to "look beautiful," were the days he rarely told me

I was. But on the days when I thought I didn't look the least bit beautiful, he would say something. One thing that used to drive me crazy was the pictures Clayton would keep of me on his phone. Clayton loves the pictures of me that I would never share or post on social media. The ones where my hair is a mess after I've been in full mom mode all day long — doing laundry, dishes, making dinner — and not a hint of makeup on my face. Clayton loves it when I wear my glasses and when my hair is slicked back, but the people who know me know that my bangs do me some good!

Though Clayton's favorite photos of me have driven me crazy, little things like that are also the very things that make me feel the most loved by him. Because he doesn't care if I'm in the best shape of my life or if I just gave birth, he just loves me without anything added or taken away.

Although I felt beautiful and outrageously loved on our wedding day, it might surprise you that the day I actually felt the most beautiful I ever have, I looked nothing like I did on the day of our wedding. I was not wearing a beautiful dress, my makeup was not done, and my hair indeed was slicked back. The day I felt the most beautiful was the day I gave birth to our daughter. Three days of back labor, 55 hours total to be exact, and I had never felt more beautiful.

Now if you saw pictures from that day, I can promise you, your first thought would not be *Wow, she's stunning.* Your first thought might actually be, *Man, she looks rough*, but I can promise you that day, the beauty I felt had nothing to do with how I looked. I felt beautiful because I had never before felt more emptied and poured out for another person. Having a baby was the most selfless thing I had ever experienced before. With every hour that passed and with every moment of longing to meet my baby, there was pain and pain and more pain . . . like I had never experienced. Yet when she came, the way I felt was something I truly could never put into words.

> **I felt beautiful because I had never before felt more emptied and poured out for another person.**

So why am I telling you about the day I gave birth and felt the most beautiful? Because I believe many of us are chasing a feeling and an approval that will never truly be enough. Whether we're aiming to impress ourselves, our friends, or our significant other, that deep satisfaction of feeling beautiful will never come from any of those people saying the perfect words. Feeling beautiful can only truly come from what is beautiful. The satisfaction I longed for most of my life came not from the words of another man, but true satisfaction came (and continues to come) when I live from what is truly beautiful — from the life of Jesus within me.

> ... true satisfaction came (and continues to come) when I live from what is truly beautiful — from the life of Jesus within me.

This world, social media, and everything in front of us every single day are telling us beauty is something to achieve. We need more clothes, we need more views, likes, and comments. All these things keep us craving more of the same. They never truly satisfy the part of a woman's heart that longs to be affirmed. What we long for from the time we're little girls is the love and approval of a loving father, yet oftentimes, we look for the satisfaction of that God-given longing in all the wrong places. Many of us have spent years hoping someone will say the words we've longed to hear, instead of realizing all the words needed have already been said.

For there is a God, a loving Father, who loved us so much that He sent His one and only Son to die, that we, as His daughters, might live! And not just live, but live abundantly. (See John 3:16; 10:10.)

The Same Love

Before I met Clayton, I was single for about two years. During those two years, I went on dates, but nothing serious. In that season of singleness, God did a lot of healing, completely wiping my memory of things I had been through and restoring my idea of "real love." Up until this point in my life, I had always separated the love of God from the love of another person. I thought the love from my husband one day would be a different love from the love I experienced from God. And this is why I got deeply confused in relationships. Yes, a man's love is not perfect, and God's love is completely perfect, but God IS love (1 John 4:8). You cannot truly know love without knowing the love of God.

I had felt for years that God would one day use my husband as the final piece of healing for my heart. In some ways, that is true, but what God really healed through my relationship with my husband was my mind. When I met Clayton, for the first time in my life, I did not feel conflicted in a relationship. I didn't feel like I was choosing the love Clayton has for me over the love God has for me because the love in which Clayton loved me was the same love I had known my entire life. Real love, the love that only comes from true love Himself.

Real love, the love that only comes from true love Himself.

To this day, I still have moments where I can feel my old view of love trying to steal the confidence in which I now live. Because the old version of love that I knew constantly needed approval. My old view of love was self-focused . . . what I looked like, what I did, how well I performed. But real love comes from a Father who says, "I am well pleased in you." You are forever approved of because Jesus was forever approved of, and you are seated with Him in heavenly places.

When you were a little girl, did you ever pick up a flower and play "He loves me, he loves me not?" If you don't know what I'm talking about, basically what you would do is pick up a flower and, one by one, pull the petals off. With each petal you pull, you say, "He loves me," or "He loves me not." And when you have pulled all the petals off, whatever it landed on, either "He loves me" or "He loves me not" is what must be true.

Sometimes I think this is how we see the love of our heavenly Father. We feel like we must constantly strive for His approval, His affection, and His attention. And when we think we're doing good in life, He must love us, but when we're not measuring up to either our standards or the standards of the world, He must love us not.

Many of us still live in this daily cycle of "He loves me, he loves me not."

Many of us are still striving to earn the attention and affirmation we think we need to be loved. But I have good news for you, daughter: you already have it! All of God's love and affection for you has been poured out through the love Jesus demonstrated on the cross. He accepted and approved of you long before you had lips, hips, and fingertips. He is in awe of what He created when He looks at you because He made you in His very own image. And because we're made in His image and His very design, our souls can only be satisfied by Him and His love for us.

Our souls can only be truly fulfilled by living from His life and love within us. God both demonstrated and freely gave true love to us through His Son Jesus. In John 15:11–13, Jesus says,

> *"These things I have spoken to you, that My joy may remain in you, and that your joy may be full. This is my commandment, that you love one another as I have loved you. Greater love has no*

one than this, than to lay down one's life for his friends" (NKJV).

1 Peter 3:3–4 says,
"Do not let your adornment be merely outward — arranging the hair, wearing gold, or putting on fine apparel — rather let it be the hidden person of the heart, with incorruptible beauty of a gentle and quiet spirit, which is very precious in the sight of God" (NKJV).

The world has lied to us about both beauty and love. Teaching us that beauty is something to achieve, so therefore, love must be achieved as well. But God made it clear to us that love is really the letting go; it's actually laying down one's life that is truly love. Beauty doesn't come from outward striving. A cute hair cut isn't bad, and by all means, wear your favorite jeans, but don't be fooled into thinking that's where your true beauty comes from, for the

Beauty doesn't come from outward striving.

life of Jesus lives within you. And He is to be praised, for He is beautiful.

When I think about the women in my life that I want to be like or that I think are absolutely stunning, I'll be honest, and I don't think any of them would be offended by this, but what I'm stunned by is not their outward beauty! Although I think they're all beautiful and have incredible features, what truly is captivating and admirable about them is who they are as people! It's the kindness in which they speak to me and others, it's how they treat me when we're together, it's the hope and joy in which they live. If they were only outwardly beautiful, yet every time we spent time together, they were mean to me, I wouldn't admire them so much. Because what is truly beautiful comes from within.

Your true identity is beautiful. In fact, I think everyone could agree that there is something about a woman who knows who they are that is incredibly captivating. Many times, as women, when we see another woman living from this kind

What is truly beautiful comes from within.

of assurance and rest within herself, we think to ourselves, "I want that."

The truth is . . .
Daughter, you have it. The beauty you long for,
desire, and admire in others is already within you.
Because the life of Jesus in your heart is what
makes you truly beautiful.

Chapter 8
Seeing the Gold

A regular, reoccurring prayer most of my life was for good friends. Growing up, being homeschooled was a huge blessing in so many ways. In fact, I loved being homeschooled, but it did bring an extra challenge when it came to making friends. If you're into the Enneagram, I'm a six. If you don't know what that means, it just means I'm loyal to the core. If we're friends in one season, I plan to be friends for life. I didn't recognize this about myself as a kid, so often I would go to extra-curricular activities and think I had made a best friend, when really for that person, I was more of an acquaintance. I loved making friends, having friends, and being a friend, but often I longed and prayed for a circle of friends where I felt like I belonged and could be fully myself!

When I moved to Nashville, God abundantly answered a prayer that I had been praying most of my life. While dancing on tour, I met my friend Sadie. I'll never forget that moment (in a non-glamorous way, might I add), in a dressing room backstage at the beginning of a tour. I walked in as she was doing her preshow warm-up dance (even though she was speaking on the tour), and before I knew it, we were both sitting on the floor bawling our eyes out, sharing some of the deepest parts of our story. I've never made a friend so quickly, yet when I look back, I think the reason that happened so fast was because we both felt like we had nothing to hide. We were both open with where we had been and what we had walked through. Turns out, we had both just come out of long-term relationships that had a whole lot of similarities. I was in a season where I really needed a good friend, and she was right there with me in her own season of needing a friend.

When I look back on that season, I've often thought I don't know what I would've done without her friendship. I know it was the kindness of Jesus loving me, leading me, and helping me. Oftentimes she spoke the very same things to me that I was already hearing from God, yet I needed a friend who could remind me what was true and walk with me through the moments that weren't "pretty." In fact, she saw me in probably the lowest moments of my life. And although

> **Oftentimes she spoke the very same things to me that I was already hearing from God, yet I needed a friend who could remind me what was true and walk with me through the moments that weren't "pretty."**

Sadie was able to comfort me because she had just walked through a similar season of her own, when I look back at this season, what I love so much is that we comforted each other, yet we didn't comfort each other to stay in the same place. Instead, we said to each other: "Let's run towards freedom, towards Jesus, and all that He has for us!"

During the tour Sadie and I were on together, we had off days in Franklin, Tennessee. Somehow, on our off days, God continued to blow us away with incredible new friendships. One day, I remember sitting in our living room on our couch, that we called "the pit," and looking up at a group of friends like I had never had in my life. I was truly overwhelmed with God's faithfulness through my friends. I guess I forgot to mention Sadie and I were roommates by this point. Eating ice cream every night was probably not the best idea, but our souls were thriving and our hearts were more free than they had ever been.

After a few months, we met our new best friends, Sarah and Gracie. And this is where God continues to use my friends to change my life! To know Sarah and Gracie is to not just love them, but to know how much they love you! When I met S and G — they're sisters, by the way — I had never met people who talked so fondly, so lovingly, and with such kindness about every single person they knew or didn't know for that matter! A reoccurring phrase out of their mouth was "They're gold." I remember thinking one day, *Do they say that about everyone? And if they say that about everyone, how could that be true?*

But as I got to know these sisters and as we did life together, became roommates, and went through many different seasons, I learned that they really meant it when they called someone "gold." And not only did they mean it, but I learned that it was true. Because, as you can imagine, if they were calling everyone gold, they were also calling me gold. This thought and continuing to hear them say this about other people, including myself, dramatically impacted the way I saw myself, saw other people, and even saw the love that God has for us. The more I was around them, the more I effortlessly began to love other people, because as I began to see gold in myself, I began to see gold in every single person.

> The more I was around them, the more I effortlessly began to love other people, because as I began to see gold in myself, I began to see gold in every single person.

And my goodness, isn't that so much of the gospel? If, while we were still sinners, Christ died for us, He must have considered us gold. He must have seen us as treasure, something worth a whole, whole lot.

Carry Them to the Healer

Your circle, who you surround yourself with, just might change your life. There's a story in Mark 2 about a paralytic man. In this story, Jesus is preaching in someone's house. The house is completely full, people are blocking the doorways, there's no way in, and there's no more room for anyone else. Yet this man is outside, being carried by four of his friends, and they're determined to get him in the house and before Jesus. So what do these four friends do? They climb on top of the house, break open the roof, and let him down on a stretcher right in the middle of the room where Jesus stood. We aren't told exactly who these four men are in relation to the paralytic, but talk about some good friends. Talk about seeing the gold. This man was helpless in his own strength, yet when he couldn't stand, when he couldn't walk, when he couldn't make it to Jesus on his own, these four friends carried him there.

That day, in the living room of a packed house, these friends were determined to carry this man to the Healer. I love this story:

When Jesus came back to Capernaum a few days later, it was heard that He was at home. And many were gathered together, so that there was no longer space, not even near the door; and He was speaking the word to them. And some people came, bringing to Him a man who was paralyzed, carried by four men. And when they were unable to get to Him because of the crowd, they removed the roof above Him; and after digging an opening, they let down the pallet on which the paralyzed man was lying. And Jesus, seeing their faith, said to the paralyzed man, "Son, your sins are forgiven." But some of the scribes were sitting there and thinking it over in their hearts, "Why does this man speak that way? He is blaspheming! Who can forgive sins except God alone?" Immediately Jesus, aware in His spirit that they were thinking that way within themselves, said to them, "Why are you thinking about these things in your hearts? Which is easier, to say to the paralyzed man, 'Your sins are forgiven'; or to say, 'Get up, and pick up your pallet and walk'? But so that you may know that the Son of Man has authority on earth to forgive sins" — *He said to the paralyzed man, "I say to you, get up, pick up your pallet, and go home." And he got up and immediately picked up the pallet and went out in the sight of everyone, so that they were all amazed and were glorifying God, saying, "We have never seen anything like this!"* (Mark 2:1–12, NASB)

I cannot count the amount of times my friends have carried me. Not physically on a stretcher, but sometimes in moments where my heart felt like it needed one. The amount of times they've picked me up and reminded me what is true by simply carrying me back to what He has said. In these four men, we see such a beautiful picture of how your circle of friends could change your life as you know it. For this man had known what it was like to have no physical strength; he had known what it was to need to be carried absolutely everywhere he went, until one day, when he couldn't have made it in the house on his own,

His friends brought him to his healing and a new way of life.

his friends brought him there. His friends brought him to his healing and a new way of life.

When It Gets Extra Fun

One of the most satisfying and fulfilling parts of being a daughter is getting to live and love other people from that position, knowing you are the treasured gold of your loving Father. Receiving that truth for yourself is what happens first and is incredibly necessary, but I have also found that getting to be that friend who carries their friends to the Healer is when it gets extra fun.

I've also found with women of every age and generation that friendships can be tough to make and to keep. I think the enemy hates when women thrive together because we can be explosive bombs when we aren't thriving. But what causes us not to thrive?

To be honest, I've had my share of explosive bombs. I've been in friendships that I thought surely would last forever, until they didn't, and I was heartbroken. I've walked through really hard moments and hard conversations in friendships, sometimes making it through and sometimes not. I've seen my friends walk through very painful and unexpected moments with their friends. It would be no new news for me to tell you that friendships can be tough, take work, and sometimes leave you heart-broken, but in an effort to possibly save you some heartache, I thought I'd share with you why I think there are too many friendships hurting and often not enough thriving.

It all starts with how we see ourselves. Friendships are made when two people get to know each other, but when we don't know ourselves, it makes this process incredibly difficult. When I say "We don't know ourselves," I'm not talking about what our enneagram number is, I'm not talking about our favorite food, our birthday, or what we do for fun. I'm talking about who we are as the trea-sured gold of our loving Father. Oftentimes we get into friendships, and we start thinking and dwelling on what our friends think about us more than we're dwell-ing on how deeply we're loved by our truest friend and good Father. This easily creates a recipe for disaster. We lose ourselves often trying to find our personality or win the approval of our friends, rather than letting our personality be shaped by the person of Jesus and His love for us.

Oftentimes we get into friendships, and we start thinking and dwelling on what our friends think about us more than we're dwelling on how deeply we're loved by our truest friend and good Father.

Since I was a little girl, I've never liked anything that seemed fake. I wasn't easily amused or fooled. I wanted the full truth and nothing but the truth when it came to Santa and the Tooth Fairy. I wouldn't play pretend, because why would I pretend when that's not real? I guess you could say it's how I'm wired, but I've always wanted "the real thing." In friendships, I've always wanted the real thing as well. I didn't want to just be friends, but I would say, "Let's be an open book, raw, and honest with each other." Then we're best friends. I don't do halfway well; if we're going to be friends, let's be friends for life. This part of my heart can also cause me to be a little more skeptical when it comes to choosing who those friends are in my life. I'll be honest and say sometimes I'm a little too skeptical, but I'm learning, and I have friends who help me with that!

When I look back on friendships I've had and even friendships I've witnessed my friends go through, whether they thrived or bombed, both seem to have a common thread. *Lies end friendships, and truth builds them.* The lies of the enemy, the lies we often listen to about ourselves, or the lies we listen to about our friends tear friendships apart, but the truth of Jesus builds friendships that stand the test of time, the changes of seasons, and miles of distance.

Lies end friendships, and truth builds them.

Notice that the lies the enemy uses to tear down a friendship aren't typically lies about the friendship but more specifically lies about each individual person in the friendship. What the enemy is still coming after in your friendships is your identity. The enemy comes after who you believe you are. And this is why we need friends, and we need to be friends who *see the gold*.

I've watched friendships start off seemingly healthy and thriving, and then suddenly one day there's a bomb, something blows up, or something comes to the surface that they've felt they needed to hide. I've watched friends start off a friendship incredibly secure and confident around another friend, and then gradually witness how they became incredibly insecure, striving for approval and acceptance. But if I could be like your best friend or sister in this moment, I want to remind you that no friend should have that kind of power over you. Your friends can lead you, remind you, and even carry you back to what is true, but your security is in Jesus, and your identity is found in His love for you.

Your friends can lead you, remind you, and even carry you back to what is true, but your security is in Jesus, and your identity is found in His love for you.

What is so beautiful about the friends God has brought into my life and what makes the story of the paralytic man so powerful is not simply my friends alone or the men who carried the paralytic, but the fact that they brought us to Jesus! And when you see yourself as gold, as a beloved daughter of your heavenly Father, you will naturally begin to do this for your friends. Seeing yourself as the treasure that you are will completely change the way you see other people and build friendships.

One of the things I love about the story of the paralytic man is that, though this man was paralyzed, his friends still believed he could be made well. His condition was no secret to them, but they believed the truth that Jesus could heal his body.

His condition was no secret to them, but they believed the truth that Jesus could heal his body.

Maybe, like it once was for me, this prayer for real, authentic, deep friendships has been a desire of your heart for a long time. Maybe, like me, you've walked through some pretty painful moments within a friendship or struggled to find your "circle." First, I want to encourage you by letting you know you're not alone in that. So many women are praying and longing for the exact same thing that you are. Secondly, like my friends have taught me, I want to encourage you to see the gold — in yourself and other people. When you begin a friendship, if you know who you are and you know you don't have to strive for approval or acceptance, your friendships will be set up to thrive. And when you believe what is true about your friends, under the blood of Jesus, you will be amazed at what God can do.

Daughter, you are gold! Not because of what you have done, but because of what He has done. Receive that truth over your heart today.

No matter what
your story is, God
so *loves* you . . .

Chapter 9
One and Only

Many people think they know a lot about God. Many people think they understand Him, can predict His every move, and interpret His heart. But many people have also done and said things in the name of Jesus that were far from His heart for the world. If you didn't grow up in church, you might feel like Christians can make church and Christianity seem like an invitation-only club or like you have to clean up your life before you are invited in. But I want to remind you of one of the most famous verses in the Bible of all time. And I also want to include the verse that follows that scripture, even though we often don't include it in our Bible lessons.

John 3:16 says, and this is good news, so get ready! *"For God **so loved the world** that He gave His only begotten Son, that whoever believes in Him*

*should not perish but have **everlasting life.***"
Continuing on to verse 17, *"For God did not
send His Son into the world to condemn the
world, but that **the world** through Him might
be saved"* (Emphasis added, NKJV).

Here's where we often get it wrong: whether we
feel like we're inside the club or whether we feel like
we're outside the club, somehow we miss the fact
that Jesus Himself said He came for **"the world"**
because He **"so loved the world."** John 3:16 doesn't
tell us that He loved only people who seemed "good,"
it doesn't say He loved people who didn't sin as much,
and it doesn't even say He only came for those who
would believe, but He came for "the world," because
He **loved** the world.

No matter what your story is, God **so loves** you
that He gave His one and only son to **die** for **you**, not
so that you would feel condemned, but that you might
believe in His love for you and experience eternal life!

The news about Jesus is good news! The news of
the gospel is good news! The news about a Father
who loves you so much that He gave His one and

only Son to die for you so that you could live is GOOD NEWS!

Having a daughter now, a "one and only" child, has given me a whole new perspective of God's love for me. One and only love is a different kind of love because they're your "one and only." I had never thought about it like this before having a child of my own, but when you have a one and only, you will do **anything** for that one and only. You will do anything to protect them, to take care of them, to heal them, to be whatever it is they need, and let's be honest, to give them everything their heart desires.

Whether you have children of your own or not, we all have someone in our lives who is our "one and only." Whether it's your spouse, your mom, your dad, your one and only sibling, or a grandparent, I think we all have experienced this "one and only" kind of love in some way or another. One and only love is special, yet sometimes I don't think we realize that is the kind of love with which our good Father loves us. He loves us like we're His one and only.

In John 15:9, Jesus said, *"As the Father loved me, I also have loved you; abide in My love"* (NKJV). I read this verse a few months ago, and it touched my heart in such a deep way. Thinking about Jesus loving me with the same love that the Father loved Him is hard to comprehend, yet this is the love we get to live in every single day as daughters and those who have the position of His one and only.

You might be thinking, *But how could God love me with this one and only love when there are billions of people in the world and God also said that He came for and loved the whole world?*

Growing up, I was the youngest of four kids. My brothers and sister were all deeply loved by my parents. When I look back, I can't see them playing "favorites," but somehow, I think I always believed I was their favorite. Somehow, I always believed I got special liberties because I saw myself as their favorite, yet looking back, it was pretty even.

Could it be that, often, the measure of love we receive is based on something we have believed?

If you read John's Gospel, you might notice that he refers to himself many times as "the disciple whom Jesus loved." I used to read that and feel sorry for the other disciples, thinking it must've been hard to not be as loved as John was by Jesus, until one day I realized that was John talking about himself. John believed he was the one whom Jesus loved. It might even be safe to say that John truly believed he was Jesus' favorite! Yet this wasn't because Jesus didn't love all the others, John just believed that Jesus really loved him.

Your belief in the richness and fullness of God's deep love for you could change your life. God's love for you never changes, whether you believe in it or not. God's love for you is rich, expansive, inclusive, far-reaching, and pouring out for you, no matter if you ever receive it or not. But what if you believed that He really loves you as His one and only? What if you saw yourself as the one that He loves? This belief and this truth

> **Your belief in the richness and fullness of God's deep love for you could change your life. God's love for you never changes, whether you believe in it or not.**

could heal your entire view of yourself. This love could heal your family, your marriage, your body, your mind, and your soul. This love is what makes the news about Jesus GOOD NEWS!

He's a Good Father

Your view of God and His heart for you could have been dramatically impacted by someone in your life. Whether it be your own father, a pastor, a friend you once had, or even a church, many things can shape our view of God and therefore, our view of ourselves. Some of these people may have impacted your life in such a beautiful way, and some, you might say, you're still trying to forgive. Wherever you are currently, I know despite what you may have been told or shown about God, He is really good, and He cares about you so much that He will heal those wounds with His love.

Being the youngest of four kids in our family, in my teenage years, I felt like I got a lot of special time with my dad when the other kids had either moved out or gone off to college. My dad and I have always been really silly when we're together. We always loved to team up on my mom and pick on her or walk funny through a mall just to see what kind of looks we could get. We had a song that was in a completely different language that we made "our song," yet to this day I still have no idea what the song was saying! We've always just liked to have fun.

Every Christmas Eve, my dad and I had a tradition of going to shop for my mom together. Though we loved to pick on her, we both just really love my mom. This became my favorite tradition and one of the only traditions that has stuck through me getting married and having a child of my own. We both have always treasured the time together and just spending the day with no agenda really, but just being together and shopping for mom.

In the last few years, I took notice of something that I had never really noticed before. I realized that when I'm with my dad, I revert back to my childhood self in a way. Suddenly, it feels like I don't really have any cares or worries. In a way, my heart and mind revert back to the way they thought when I was a child, completely carefree. As a kid, when I was with my dad, I knew I was protected, I knew I was taken care of, I knew I was provided for, and I knew I was loved.

You may be reading this right now and you feel like you can't relate to my relationship with my dad at all. Maybe your dad made you feel the complete opposite of this, maybe he was absent, or maybe you never got to meet your dad. I want you to know that though my earthly story has been different and my heart sympathizes with yours, in light of forever and eternity, our story is the same. For there is a loving Father who loved you and me so much that He called us His very own. There is a God and a good Father who is close to us, who protects us, takes care of us, provides for us, and heals us. See, the reason I feel this way with my dad is simply because he has received the love the Father has for him, and now he lives from that love. And because he has received that love, I have been a recipient of that love.

Although I know and believe my dad is amazing, I also know that it's not simply him alone that makes him what he is to me. The goodness and kindness of our heavenly Father who has loved my dad, has made him who he is and the incredible father that he has been. If my dad didn't believe that his heavenly Father was taking care of him, protecting him, and providing for him, I don't think I would have received those things from him as his child. But in my dad, I have seen the love of my heavenly Father and the trust of a child.

> **If my dad didn't believe that his heavenly Father was taking care of him, protecting him, and providing for him, I don't think I would have received those things from him as his child.**

Like a Child

In Matthew 19:14, Jesus told His disciples, *"Let the little children come to me and do not hinder them, for to such belongs the kingdom of heaven"* (ESV). In Matthew 18, the disciples came to Jesus, asking Him who was the greatest in the kingdom of heaven. Jesus called over a child, put him in the midst of them, and said, *"Truly, I say to you, unless you turn and become like children, you will never enter the kingdom of heaven.*

Whoever humbles himself like this child is the greatest in the kingdom of heaven" (v. 3–4, ESV).

The world we live in can often make us feel like we need to get all of our stuff figured out before we can come to God. Oftentimes, following Jesus is portrayed to us like another system to follow. One of the most asked questions I've received since I started doing "ministry" is, "How do I start reading my Bible?"

In many ways, what people are asking is, "How do I come to God?" But the reason they don't know how to come to God is because many people haven't been told, or don't realize, that they can simply come like a child. Many people don't realize that the kingdom of heaven belongs to them and they can simply come like children.

> **Many people don't realize that the kingdom of heaven belongs to them and they can simply come like children.**

Jesus said He came to give us life and life abundantly (John 10:10). What Jesus didn't say is that He also came to give us knowledge, and knowledge abundantly. One of my favorite verses as a child was 1 Corinthians 8:1–3. It says, *". . . But knowledge puffs up while love builds up. Those who think they know something do not yet know as they ought to know. But whoever loves God is known by God"* (NIV). As a kid, I loved this verse in moments when I felt like I didn't have a lot of answers. Now as an adult, I still love this verse because I've realized very few of us have a lot of answers in the grand picture of life. Yet, if I'm known by God, that is more than enough for me.

There is great freedom in coming to our loving heavenly Father like the child we were always meant to be. Although knowledge could tell you some

There is great freedom in coming to our loving heavenly Father like the child we were always meant to be.

things about God, I can promise you that coming to Him like a child will tell you a whole lot more. For the kingdom of heaven belongs to children.

Many believers today still have trouble when it comes to reading their Bible. In fact, I've gone through my own seasons of feeling almost a sense of resentment towards reading my Bible. But the reason I believe we either live in this place or only visit it is because we often forget how He told us to come to Him. Many times, we open our Bible and put the pressure on ourselves to do the work, to gain more knowledge, or receive something from Him. Yet, we miss that JESUS called the children to Himself, HE set the child in His midst,

Many times, we open our Bible and look for ourselves, what we need to do, or what we can improve. But when you begin to look for Jesus in His Word, I believe you will naturally begin to see yourself in the light of the way that He sees you.

and HE spoke inheritance, identity, and belonging over the child. All the child did was come. And that remains our part today. Jesus draws us in, and we get to come as His children and the ones that He loves.

If you find yourself in this place, wanting to read your Bible but not knowing where to start, I want to encourage you with what someone encouraged me with years ago . . . "When you open your Bible, look for Jesus." This may not seem super profound, but it completely changed the way I saw and read Scripture. Many times, we open our Bible and look for ourselves, what we need to do, or what we can improve. But when you begin to look for Jesus in His Word, I believe you will naturally begin to see yourself in the light of the way that He sees you. And on an even more practical note, start with one verse. Find one verse that speaks to your heart and dwell on that verse for the entire week.

I fell in love with reading my Bible as a child. Not because anyone made me, but because even at a young age, I began to deal with such intense fear. Every night when I would go to bed and turn the light out, it would feel like someone set a ton of bricks on my chest. The fear and anxiety felt all consuming. One night, instead of trying to fight it on my own, I went down to my mom's bedroom and told her what I was experiencing. She looked at me, half asleep, and said, "Laney, breathe Jesus." I went back up to my room, sat on my bed, and began breathing the name of Jesus out loud. I'll never forget this moment because it was one of the first moments I experienced God's tangible presence with me. There was a supernatural peace and stillness that washed over my chest, and if I stop and think back — I can almost feel what I felt that day because it was so tangible.

From that moment, I started reading my Bible at night before I would go to bed. I read Psalm 3:5 over and over: *"I lay down and slept, yet I woke up in safety, for the LORD was watching over me"* (NLT). I began literally laying my head on my Bible like a pillow at night because I had experienced such a deep, tangible love from my Father. I wasn't reading my Bible to gain more knowledge, I was reading my Bible because I felt really loved by my heavenly Father.

So, daughter, when you come to Him, come as you are. If you're broken, come broken, because He's the healer. If you're scared, come scared, because His perfect love drives out fear. If you're feeling hopeless, come to Him feeling hopeless, for He will fill you with the hope that He is.

You are His child, and you can come as you are.

"Fear not, for I am with you; be not dismayed, for I am your God. I will strengthen you, Yes, I will help you, I will uphold you with My righteous right hand" (Isaiah 41:10, NKJV).

Chapter 10
In-Security

As a young teenager, I was a part of a Christian choir that sang and danced. I joined a choir initially because I wanted to dance, but later realized part of the reason I wanted to dance was because I believed I couldn't sing. So I thought that by dancing in a choir, where people couldn't actually hear me, I could fulfill my desire to sing as well. One day, after a couple years of dancing with this choir, the choir director pulled me into her office and asked me about singing a solo. The solo she asked me to sing was a song called "Lamb of God" [5] in a large theater performance we had coming up. She prefaced her ask by telling me she had recently had a dream about me singing this song that night. Although when she asked me, the thought was a bit terrifying because, in that season,

I did not sing in front of people, something in my 14-year-old self was also thrilled.

As time passed and we got closer to our "big performance," we began having rehearsals. I had been practicing this song at home for months and had imagined myself singing with such confidence, but as the time came for me to sing in front of all my peers in the choir, something came over me that I hadn't felt in my bedroom singing the song all by myself. My palms got sweaty, I started to shake, and I was trying to sing and project, but it was as if someone had turned the volume off on my voice. As I held the microphone, I remember thinking, "I don't even know how to hold this thing," a thought I had not had to worry about the whole time up until that point. All of a sudden, I was incredibly nervous and unsure of what everyone around me was thinking. After I had sung a verse and a chorus, the choir director turned off the music and said, "Laney, you just need more confidence."

Looking back now, it was pretty obvious. Of course, I needed more confidence! I was terrified! But telling someone they need more confidence when they're feeling insecure does not instantly instill confidence. Just like when someone is completely overwhelmed with fear, telling them the Bible says, "Do not fear," will not instantly take away their fear. Both instances are missing a very key factor. "Do not fear" is the most often used command in the Bible, yet it is almost always followed with why we do not have to fear.

Isaiah 41:10 says, *"Fear not, for I am with you; be not dismayed, for I am your God. I will strengthen you, Yes, I will help you, I will uphold you with My righteous right hand"* (NKJV).

As a young girl, a teenager, and even into my twenties, I desperately desired to have confidence. I wanted to not worry what other people thought about me. But simply telling myself every day to not worry about what other people think did not take away my fear of what other people thought. Insecurity, according to the dictionary is defined as a state or feeling of anxiety, fear, or self-doubt. [6]

I have to be honest with you; though I feel confident and secure most days of my life, it's not because I have zero self-doubt. In fact, I've got plenty of reasons ready to go of why I should still doubt myself to this day. I could doubt my abilities, I could doubt my own strength, I could doubt my appearance, the way I look, or the clothes I choose to wear. I could doubt my knowledge or my ability to communicate. Looking at myself and myself alone gives me many reasons to doubt myself. But the Bible does not define confidence and security the same way the dictionary does.

> **Looking at myself and myself alone gives me many reasons to doubt myself. But the Bible does not define confidence and security the same way the dictionary does.**

Proverbs 14:26 says, *"In the fear of the LORD is strong confidence, and His children will have a place of refuge"* (NKJV). And Psalm 118:8 says, *"It is better to trust in the LORD, than to put confidence in man"* (NKJV).

Though your soul longs for a place to rest securely, you will not find that rest within yourself. Your freedom, confidence, and security will not come from you not doubting yourself, for there will always be something you could find about yourself that is insecure and insufficient in your own strength. But you will be filled by true confidence and security when you embrace your frailty, when you admit you have desperate needs, and when you bring those insecurities to a secure Father who makes you whole.

But you will be filled by true confidence and security when you embrace your frailty, when you admit you have desperate needs, and when you bring those insecurities to a secure Father who makes you whole.

We're All Desiring the Same Thing

My mom is a mother of four children. Now that we're all married and have children of our own, she has about 17 of us that she mothers and grandmothers. She was a stay-at-home mom, but don't let that fool you. Having one child of my own is a full-time job, so I can only imagine what it was like to be home with all of us each day and homeschool all four at the same time. My mom is the one who, in many ways, showed me who I wanted to be when I grew up. Mom always had a verse or a song ready to go to show us how good God is to us. She taught me, but mostly she showed me what it looked like to trust Him, like really trust Him. On what I thought was a bad day, mom could always turn it around to make it look like something good. Mom was confident, secure, and sure of her role as a mom and a wife to my dad. I always knew, because she told us, that she was getting to do what she always dreamed of by being our mom, and she still is to this day.

Mom is now a confident mother-in-law and grandma, and she owns her roles very well. Beautifully. With grace and a loose grip. I think I can speak for all of her children and grandchildren when I say that we all feel free around her. She is love with no expectation of anything in return . . . which makes us love her even more.

So I asked her the other day, because I mostly see her in her comfort zone and where she feels most secure, "Mom, where do you feel the most secure and where do you feel the most insecure?" She took a moment to think about it and then said, "I think

I feel the most insecure when I feel like I have to be something I'm not." And then she said, "And I feel the most secure around other people who will admit they have needs just like I do." I loved her answer because I feel like it's relatable to literally every single one of us. We all have been in settings before or around certain people, and suddenly we feel this incredible pressure to be something we're not. We've all been in settings where we are suddenly hyper-aware of our insecurities, where we feel extremely insignificant, and like no one around us has the same needs we do. But hopefully this is some good news for you — to hear that though every woman or girl might not be willing to show you, every woman and girl has the same desperate needs that you do.

> ... every woman and girl has the same desperate needs that you do.

Just as you want to be loved, accepted, and secure, they want to be loved, accepted, and secure. We're all searching and desiring the same thing at the heart of who we are, even though we can often look for these things in different places.

So the next time you walk into a room full of women, before you allow yourself to start comparing and feeling insignificant and insecure, remember, they are all desiring the same thing you are, they may just not be as willing to show you.

JE – SUS

Thinking back to that day in that choir room, to the girl with no idea how to hold the microphone, is a wide-eyed look for me of where God has brought me from and the strength of what His love can do. If you would've told me then that I would eventually write and release songs of my own, I seriously would not have believed you.

I want you to know that my voice really hasn't changed that much since then. I didn't turn into Carrie Underwood overnight. I still have my voice. But there was a turning point, a very memorable moment for me in my life, where I stopped acting like I had it all together and began to admit that I was far, far from it. I started admitting I had flaws, even though that wasn't as big of a secret as I thought it was. I wasn't fooling other people, I was only fooling myself and making it harder on myself! Because I believed it would be better for me to act like I had it altogether than be really honest and open with the truth that I didn't.

But the reason I live confident and whole today is not because I have less of a reason to be insecure, no! No matter what you do to cover up or fix your insecurities, if it doesn't start with JE and end with SUS, it won't last. Because nothing can give you the love, acceptance, and security that your loving Father can.

> **No matter what you do to cover up or fix your insecurities, if it doesn't start with JE and end with SUS, it won't last.**

Like my mom, I would say I feel the most insecure when I feel like I have to be something I'm not. And when I feel uncomfortable or insecure, it's likely you will know because my face will turn red and I might even be visibly sweating.

I want to tell you this story, but please hear my heart in what I'm saying, because it feels a little funny for me to share it.

The way I got into what I'm doing now — writing books, singing, and speaking, sharing about the love of Jesus with people — all started from being a backup dancer, to then making funny videos that started to get really popular on social media with my best friend. When our videos started to get a lot of views, I started getting recognized some while I was out and about. Disclaimer: This is why this feels funny because I'm aware that I'm not Justin Bieber, but this was a very interesting time in my life. One of the very first times that a group of girls came up to me and my best friend in public, we still talk and laugh about it today because I was so OBVIOUSLY uncomfortable. And it wasn't because these girls said or did anything wrong, but it was clear that I was RED and sweating!

It wasn't normal for me to be put in that position. And they were asking me tons of questions, to which I felt like I had to have some special answer instead of just being me! I thought since they seemed to think I was something special, that I had to be some extra kind of special, putting pressure on myself to be something that I'm not. And truthfully, because at that time in life, I would take a hundred different pictures until I got the "perfect" one, I thought I had to make them believe once again that I was perfect. But what good does me being "perfect" do for them? They can't gain anything from me pretending to be perfect. But I have learned that I can give away so much more when I'm willing to admit that I'm not.

But what good does me being "perfect" do for them? They can't gain anything from me pretending to be perfect.

When I'm willing to admit that I have needs and that I have insecurities and flaws. When I do that, I not only free myself to be embraced by the healing love of my father, but I free other women to be embraced by the healing love of their Father.

Do you often find yourself in spaces where you feel the need to be something that you're not? Do you hear the lies that tell you, "If you're honest about your frailties, people won't truly love you?" Because

I've been there. I've heard all the lies, and I believed them for a season — for way too long of a season. What keeps us captive to our insecurities is not simply having them; it's trying to convince ourselves and others that we don't have any. The day I found confidence and true freedom was the day I came to the end of myself. The day I realized and received, *"My flesh and my heart may fail, but God is the strength of my heart and my portion forever"* (Psalm 73:26, NIV).

> **What keeps us captive to our insecurities is not simply having them; it's trying to convince ourselves and others that we don't have any.**

Daughter, His love and His faithfulness to you is where you will find the security your heart is desperately longing for. Let go. Let go of the pressure to be something you're not. Freedom is waiting for you in His arms. True confidence, rest, and assurance is yours to receive.

Chapter 11
Good, Good Gifts

I prayed for my future husband since I was a young teenager. Growing up, there was no doubt in my mind that I would get married one day. I realized as I got older that not everyone has that belief, though many women and men have that desire. I had seen my parents have a beautiful, healthy marriage. I was incredibly blessed to see my grandparents have a long, healthy marriage, and I was surrounded by many beautiful marriages on all sides of me. When I say "healthy," I do not mean perfect by any means, but I knew these marriages were built on the love of Jesus and the love He had for each individual in the marriage.

When I turned 18, I started my first dating relationship, which lasted four years. I talk about this season of my life often because, though it was full of much heartbreak, it was also the gateway to me discovering the love that Jesus had for me in its fullness. Because when I was broken, I recognized my deep, deep need for comfort, for a healer, and for redemption that only Jesus could give.

Those four years of my life were much like a roller coaster; some days were great, and some days I would never wish upon any woman. Yet all the crazy that I went through has opened a way for me to encourage and help other women going through many of the same things. I don't believe God put me in that relationship to teach me a lesson; rather, I believe I made many decisions that weren't from a place of peace. Still, God has redeemed every bad decision and every moment of heartache and gone above and beyond to answer the prayer of a little girl who desired to be married one day.

When I met Clayton and saw firsthand redemption play out in my life, I was very vocal on social media of what God had done. I wanted to shout it from every rooftop, and social media was the closest thing to a rooftop that I knew of. I'll never forget, as I began to share what God had done, the ways He redeemed what I had previously walked through, and the amazement of who the man I met was, the comments of women who said, "God doesn't promise us a husband!" They were very quick to come with a negative word, making sure I knew that "God promises every single woman a husband" was not found in the Bible.

Although it's true that I haven't found a verse that promises me and you a husband in this life, I can find plenty that promise God is good, God is faithful, and He loves to give good gifts to His children. I also believe our desire to be married is God-given. When God made Adam in Genesis 2:18, He said, *"It is not good for the man to be alone; I will make him a helper suitable for him"* (NASB).

Matthew 7:7–8 says,

"Ask and it will be given to you; seek and you will find; knock and the door will be opened to you. For everyone who ask receives; the one who seeks finds; and to the one who knocks, the door will be opened" (NIV).

This is your liberty — to come and ask Him like the child you are. Though you may not find a specific scripture in the Bible that promises you a husband, believe that if you have that desire in your heart, how much more does your good Father want to fulfill that desire and give you a good gift? Come to Him, asking, and come with faith in your heart, for He who promised He would be faithful is faithful.

Come to Him, asking, and come with faith in your heart, for He who promised He would be faithful is faithful.

I often tell people Clayton is a tangible picture of God's faithfulness to me. As a young girl and into my twenties, as I prayed for my husband, I never could've imagined the man God would give me. The gift He gave is so so much better than I could've dreamed.

After I came out of that long-term relationship, I remember the lies of the enemy becoming so loud. "No one will ever truly love you." "No one will want to be with you after you've been in a relationship that long." "You'll never find what you're truly looking for." "What you're waiting for doesn't exist." "Your standards are too high" . . . and the list goes on forever. I want you to know that it doesn't matter if you're single and in your twenties or single and above your 30s; you qualify for the blessings and redemption of the Father, and nothing is too hard or too far gone for Him to redeem.

A verse I love so much that I keep on my bathroom mirror to this day is Ephesians 3:20, it says,

"Never doubt God's mighty power to work in you and accomplish all this.

He will achieve infinitely more than your greatest request, your most unbelievable dream, and exceed your wildest imagination! He will outdo them all, for His miraculous power constantly energizes you" (TPT).

He will achieve infinitely more than your greatest request, your most unbelievable dream, and exceed your wildest imagination!

Daughter, don't doubt, for your Father is more faithful to you than you can dream. His faithfulness goes far, far beyond your own. If He has put it in your heart, trust Him to be who He is, for He is faithful to you. There's nothing you've given away and nothing that has been stolen from you that God cannot redeem. The years, the nights, the conversations, the words, the pain, the heartache . . . nothing is outside of His touch. And though it may feel contrary to how you feel, you are not far-off from your loving, redeeming Father. You're close enough to touch. He's got you in His loving arms, fully wrapped in His tender care.

What Are You Believing For?

Clayton and I had both dated people prior to dating each other, yet when we met, it felt like we were both dating for the very first time. Everything felt new, and each day we saw each other, there was such a childlike, giddy excitement . . . or at least that's how I felt! One thing that stood out to me when we started dating was the way I always had such peace when I was with him. I felt safe and at rest, like I had nothing to prove. Honestly, a very similar way to how I had always felt when I was with my dad.

One night early on in our dating relationship, Clayton asked me to go to a "writer's round" with a couple of his friends. If you don't know what a writer's round is, it's where song writers come to sing their original songs. Of course, I said yes, but when I showed up, I was met with a bit of an unexpected surprise. Turns out, his friends were both girls. Definitely didn't expect that. I found out later, apparently in college, this was normal for guys and girls to hang out and be friends and have no interest in each other, yet I'm still of the unpopular opinion that this is not super sustainable because someone typically ends up having feelings for the other person. But anyway, like I said, this was early in the relationship.

That night, as we were listening to music, I was doing my best to connect with these girls, whom I thought were some of his good friends, but getting very little in return. I started catching the wave that maybe they didn't really want to be friends with me, which definitively served my assumption that maybe one of them liked my now husband as more than a friend. Becoming very discouraged by the people I thought were his good friends having no desire to want to get to know me, I left that night pretty sad. Clayton could visibly tell something was up, so we decided to walk out early.

Before I tell you what happens next, I want to flash back to the week right before this. I was out of town with my parents; they had just moved into a new house, so they were looking for things to decorate the interior. One of the days I was with them, we were walking through a furniture store. My parents had walked into another nook of the store while I stood in the rug section. This may be strange, but I love the smell of a new rug. As I stood there, across the room was a beautiful oval mirror, and as I stared at the mirror for a couple of seconds, my dad came around beside me and hugged me. I'm not sure what it was about the way that he hugged me, but I immediately had tears streaming down my face and felt extremely loved, protected, and secure. This was not a new way of feeling around my dad, but that day, for whatever reason, I just really needed that hug.

So back to me and Clayton walking out of the "writer's round." We walked out, and Clayton could tell something was off. I was trying to be slow to speak because if those were his friends, I wanted them to be my friends too, but the truth is that night, I did not feel welcomed there. I was used to the friends I was around being overly kind and welcoming, and instead it just felt like there was competition for whatever reason in the air.

When Clayton saw the look on my face and could tell that my countenance was down, he immediately threw his arms around me the exact same way my dad had the week before. And I immediately felt that same love, protection, and security.

So why am I telling you this? What does this have to do with you being a daughter? I'm sharing this with you because I know I'm not the only one who has asked for things and then wondered if I was wrong for asking. I know I'm not the only one who has longed for a husband

I know I'm not the only one who has longed for a husband and gotten extremely discouraged in the waiting.

and gotten extremely discouraged in the waiting. And when people came to me saying, "Laney, God didn't promise us a husband," I had to do some asking and seeking because I knew the man I was given was too good for my own efforts or searching out. I knew God had been faithful, and God had given me one heck of a gift in my husband. And I would like to be so bold as to say that I believe that God is more faithful to give to you than you are faithful to ask of Him. He loves to give good gifts to His daughters. And you will be amazed at the width, depth, and detail of how He can fill and redeem your story.

> . . . I believe that God is more faithful to give to you than you are faithful to ask of Him. He loves to give good gifts to His daughters.

Ask, Seek, Knock

Before Clayton came into my life, God had already done worlds of healing in my heart and mind. I was beginning to see how speaking of His faithfulness did

148

wonders in my life. Though some of these moments were on a podcast, it was the private moments in my apartment that truly changed the reality of what I lived in each day. I remember many times after my three roommates would leave, I would grab my Bible and stand in the middle of our kitchen and read a verse or passage over myself that I was clinging to for dear life! One of the passages that I still speak over myself often, and we have painted on a canvas in our living room today, is from Psalm 18:1–3. This passage became a foundation for me and built great confidence in my soul of who this God and Father is that I had believed in my whole life.

It says,

"I love you, Yahweh, and I'm bonded to you, my strength! Yahweh, you're the bedrock beneath my feet, my faith-fortress, my wonderful deliverer, my God, my rock of rescue where none can reach me. You're the shield around me, the mighty power that saves me, and my high place. All I need to do is call on you, Yahweh, the praise-worthy God. When I do, I'm safe and sound in you — delivered from my foes!" (TPT).

I memorized this verse so that I could whip it out when I need it, which is often. This world and its frailties can feel overwhelming at times, but this verse has reminded me that God alone is my foundation, the bedrock beneath my feet, and my true hope.

Speaking life over my mind, my heart, and my body has changed my life in more ways than I can count or recall. Proverbs 4:22 tells us that our Father's words to us *"are life to those who find them, and health to all their flesh"* (NKJV). Proverbs 18:21 tells us that our words have *"the power of life and death"* (NIV).

When we have walked through heartache in life, it's easy to expect more heartache or begin to speak more heartache over our future. But just because you've walked through something painful in the past does not disqualify you from the redemption and goodness that your Father has stored up for you.

It's time for you to believe that your good Father is truly good! And it's time for you to speak of it.

It's time for you to believe that your good Father is truly good! And it's time for you to speak of it. Don't let the broken things of the past or painful circumstances you've walked through tell you who your Father is; let your good, loving heavenly Father tell you who He is. Let Him redeem what you've walked through and start believing that He really does desire to give you good, good gifts!

You may be happily married, but you've been wondering if it's biblical to ask or believe God for blessings in your life. Maybe like me, someone has told you that God doesn't promise you what it is you've been asking and believing for. Though it may not look how you thought or expected, you can know that what is in His heart for you is so much better than what's even in your heart for yourself. His dreams and plans for you are so much better than you could come up with on your own. So why shouldn't you ask? Why shouldn't you believe? For you can ask and believe from a place of knowing "how much more" your Father will give good gifts to those who ask of Him. "How much more" is His heart for you. He has more for you than you can even begin to imagine.

Daughter, whatever it is that's on your heart and on your mind right now . . . whisper it. Begin speaking — out loud — of His faithfulness to you and declare the promise that "He works all things for the good of those who love Him" over your life today. I believe you will begin to experience His goodness and His heart for you in a way that you never have before.

Chapter 12

What You Believe

Let's talk about what you believe.

There are so many things that play into what you believe and why you believe it. Millions of thoughts have impacted your views and beliefs about a million different things. In fact, you believe things that you don't even consciously know you believe. You believe things about yourself, things about God, and things about other people, whether good or bad, true or not true. You have many subconscious beliefs that come out in the choices you make every day. Of course, you have some things that, if I asked you, you wouldn't know how to say what it is you believe, and there may even be things that you change your mind on while you're trying to explain your belief, but bottom line, what you believe is so incredibly important because ultimately, what you believe will direct the path of your life.

This became a reality for me when my life wasn't going the way I hoped it would, and I began searching for change. I didn't know initially what kind of change I needed, but realized later that God wanted to heal, restore, and completely change the way I believed about many things.

. . . God wanted to heal, restore, and completely change the way I believed about many things.

Growing up, I was "a good kid." I didn't get in trouble much, definitely less than my siblings, and so in my eyes, I was doing pretty good. I believed in Jesus from a young age, but my belief in Jesus has dramatically changed since I was a child. In some areas, I want to believe more like I did as a child, and in other areas, I'm incredibly grateful that His grace has radically changed how I think since I was a child.

A subconscious thought for me as a kid, without sugar coating it, was that I was better than other people. In my eyes, though I knew I needed Jesus, I still thought other people needed Him more because their sin seemed to be more visible. Now as an adult, I consciously know that I NEED HIM even more than everyone else. I mean, I know we all need Him, but God has met me in such a way that I have no doubt that I really, really need Him, just as much as we all do. There is no meter, no measure, of who needs His grace more, because we all desperately need it. Without His grace, there wouldn't be a gospel. Without His grace, we would not have the hope of salvation. Our righteousness, without the blood of Jesus covering us, is nothing. And that is why we are all desperate for His grace that He has given as a free gift to those who believe.

I'll never forget the moment when the reality that I had this subconscious belief was brought to my attention. I remember talking to my mom one day about a friend who had done something "bad." In my eyes at the time, they had committed a horrible sin. And subconsciously, I began to look at them differently. I had trouble seeing my friend without thinking about what they had done. Maybe you can relate to this? And as I sat across from my mom, explaining my thought process, she looked at me and said, "Laney, your righteousness is no greater than theirs . . . It's the same blood." She went on to explain what she meant by that, and as she continued, I remember just having a complete reality check. It was a moment of realizing that I had really believed that other people needed the blood of Jesus more than I did, and man, that could not be further from the truth.

This is just one example of many beliefs God has changed, shifted, and completely rewired over the course of my life. He has changed my mind and my heart a million ways and a million different times. And to be honest, I pray He never stops changing me, that I'm always learning new things about who He is and seeing more of the extravagant love He has poured out for us. Growing and changing, rewiring, believing new things about Him, and oftentimes uprooting old things we have believed about Him is just part of the journey. It's part of growing and being His daughter. Although telling you that I used to have a subconscious belief that I was better than other people is not something I'm proud of, I also have no shame in sharing that with you because of what God has done in my heart since then.

Uprooting beliefs that aren't true of who God is or who you are is always a good thing. I used to feel the pressure to have all the answers about what I believe about every little thing, but I've realized now that I had an impossible expectation on myself. I'm not God, therefore I will never have all the answers, but allowing yourself to admit that positions you to be led and changed by Him. Admitting you're wrong in ways that you don't even know you're wrong will allow space in your mind and heart to hear Him speak to you about those things that you may not even know you have wrongly believed about who He is or who you are.

I'm not God, therefore I will never have all the answers, but allowing yourself to admit that positions you to be led and changed by Him.

God Box

Have you ever heard the term "God box" before? This may be a super "churchy" term; I'm honestly not even sure where I first heard it, but basically, your "God box" is an imaginary box where all the things you believe about God go. Whether you believe in God or whether you don't believe in God. All the things you believe about Him and all the things you don't believe about Him. What you believe about yourself regarding how you see God and what you don't believe about yourself because of how you see God. Basically, it's a box full of beliefs, or unbeliefs. And for those of you who say, "Don't put God in a box," you are correct; it's never a good idea, but we all do it in our own way.

But the question I really want to ask you is this: are you willing to admit that there are some things in your God box, subconsciously or consciously, that are possibly not true? Would you be willing to admit that maybe you've believed some things about God, possibly from the time you were a little girl, that aren't even close to true of His heart for you?

So often we walk through things and circumstances that we can't make sense of, and then those things shape our beliefs about who God is. Oftentimes, our view of God is shaped more by our world than by God Himself, what He said, and the way He showed Himself to us through the person of Jesus.

Many people today still don't believe it's God's heart to heal. I can't explain every story to you; I don't know why I've walked through some of the pain I have and seen other people go through, but when I look at Jesus, I see that He healed people! I see that was His heart; He stopped, completely re-routed His trips, and changed His plans to step in the house of a sick person to heal them. When I look at how He made our bodies, when I think on the truth that I'm made in His image, and when I scrape my knee and watch how it heals itself, I can't deny His desire and His nature is to heal.

Again, so many things shape our beliefs. I know you've been through some things and seen some things that I probably couldn't explain or understand on this side of heaven either. But I know that He promises you that He's good and that He works all things for your good. Maybe He wants to show you a completely new way of looking at what you've walked through. What if, in that moment of your

What if, in that moment of your life when you were convinced He wasn't there, He actually was there? life when you were convinced He wasn't there, He actually was there? And maybe he wants to show you his goodness even in a moment that you thought was the worst day of your life. I know that He can, because He's done that for me in my own life.

You might even be in a place where you need to completely start over with what you put in your "God box," and there is no shame in that. Because if that is the case, you will look back one day and tell the story about how you once believed what you believed and tell it without even an ounce of shame. Because when God rewires and heals the way we think and believe, it produces such bubbling over, life-giving freedom without any shame for who we used to be or how we used to think.

The best way to discover where we aren't believing what is true is by discovering what is true. And the Bible is the best place to discover what is true. When I find myself questioning His faithfulness,

I read about His faithfulness. When I find myself doubting His promises to me, I read what He has promised. When I feel fearful, I read about His love for me because I know His perfect love drives out all fear. No matter how we have believed what isn't true, there is a truth for that very area found in His word.

So if I can, I want to help you start believing what is true about God by giving you some foundational scriptures for you to cling to. You may not know what all belongs in your "God box," but in the words of John Eldridge, "If it doesn't bring freedom and it doesn't bring life, it's not Christianity." [7]

Before you continue, I want to encourage you to take your time as you read these scriptures. Don't be in a hurry, and if you dare, speak them out loud over yourself.

Jesus Is Your AUTHORITY:

"Behold, I give you the authority to trample on serpents and scorpions, and over ALL the power of the enemy, and nothing shall by any means hurt you" (Luke 10:19, NKJV).

Jesus Is Your STRENGTH:

"He gives power to the weak, and to those who have no might He increases strength. Even the youths shall faint and be weary, and the young men shall utterly fall. But those who wait on the LORD shall renew their strength; they shall mount up with wings like eagles, they shall run and not be weary, they shall walk and not faint" (Isaiah 40:29–31, NKJV).

Jesus Is Your ADVOCATE:

"My little children, these things I write to you, so that you may not sin. And if anyone sins, we have an Advocate with the Father, Jesus Christ the righteous" (1 John 2:1, NKJV).

Jesus Invites You Into His REST:

"Come to Me, all you who labor and are heavy laden, and I will give you REST. Take My yoke upon you and learn from Me, for I am gentle and lowly in heart, and you will find rest for your souls. For My yoke is easy and My burden is light" (Matthew 11:28–30, NKJV).

Jesus Is Your FREEDOM:

"Therefore if the son make you free, you shall be free indeed" (John 8:36, NKJV).

Jesus Is Your SATISFACTION:

"You open Your hand and satisfy the desire of every living thing" (Psalm 145:16, NKJV).

Jesus Is Your VICTORY:

"The sting of death is sin, and the strength of sin is the law. But thanks be to God, who gives us the victory through our Lord Jesus Christ" (1 Corinthians 15:56–57, NKJV).

Jesus Is Your DIRECTION:

"Trust in the LORD with all your heart, and lean not on your own understanding; in all your ways acknowledge Him, and He shall direct your paths" (Proverbs 3:5–6, NKJV).

Jesus Is Your QUALIFICATION:

"But God has chosen the foolish things of the world to put to shame the wise, and God has

chosen the weak things of the world to put to shame the things which are mighty; and the base things of the world and the things which are despised GOD HAS CHOSEN, and the things which are not, to bring to nothing the things that are, that no flesh should glory in His presence" (1 Corinthians 1:27–29, NKJV).

Jesus Is Your REDEEMER:

"He has sent redemption to His people; He has commanded His covenant forever: Holy and awesome is His name" (Psalm 111:9, NKJV).

Jesus Is Your DELIVERER:

"Because he has set his love upon Me, therefore I will deliver him; I will set him on high, because he has known My name. He shall call upon Me, and I will answer him; I will be with him in trouble; I will deliver him and honor him. With long life I will satisfy him, and show him My salvation" (Psalm 91:14–16, NKJV).

Jesus Is Your RIGHTEOUSNESS:

"For if by the one man's offense death reigned through the one, much more those who receive abundance of grace and of the gift of righteousness will reign in life through the One, JESUS CHRIST" (Romans 5:17, NKJV).

Jesus Gives You a SOUND MIND:

"For God has not given us a spirit of fear, but of power and of love and of a SOUND MIND" (2 Timothy 1:7, NKJV).

Jesus Is the Restorer of Your HEALTH AND YOUR HEALER:

"For I will restore health to you and heal you of your wounds," says the LORD . . . (Jeremiah 30:17, NKJV).

Jesus Is Your ACCEPTANCE:

"But God, who is rich in mercy, because of His great love with which He loved us, even when we were dead in trespasses, made us alive together with Christ (by grace you have been

saved), and raised us up together, and made us sit together in the heavenly places in Christ Jesus" (Ephesians 2:4–6, NKJV).

Jesus Is Your DEFENDER:

"So when they continued asking Him, He raised Himself up and said to them, 'He who is without sin among you, let him throw a stone at her first'" (John 8:7, NKJV).

In the story, this woman is caught in the very act of adultery, and her accusers are watching, waiting for Jesus to accuse her too, but it says Jesus defends the woman in the very act of her sin. Oftentimes we think Jesus is disappointed with us when we sin, but this is the perfect picture of what is really going on — Jesus doesn't condemn us, but He defends us and provides for us the way out.

Jesus Is Your PROTECTOR:

"The angel of the Lord encamps around those who fear him, and he delivers them" (Psalm 34:7, NIV).

"But the Lord is faithful, and he will strengthen you and protect you from the evil one" (2 Thessalonians 3:3, NIV).

"Fear not, for I am with you; be not dismayed, for I am your God. I will strengthen you, Yes, I will help you, I will uphold you with My righteous right hand" (Isaiah 41:10, NKJV).

Jesus Is Your COMFORT:
"Yea, though I walk through the valley of the shadow of death, I will fear NO evil; for You are with me; Your rod and your staff, they comfort me" (Psalm 23:4, NKJV).

Daughter, no matter where you are in believing the good news about Jesus, there is always more of Him to be discovered. Being His daughter comes without any shame of growing and learning just like a child. So let your mind be changed, let it grow, and let things shift and rearrange as He reveals more of His heart to you each day. But never stop believing that He's good, for when you know He is good, you will allow yourself to see His heart in all things.

Chapter 13

Show Me Where You Were

There's a beautiful part of being His that is really hard for me to describe in words. Yet today I want to try, because I know the hope that is buried beneath my lack of words could be the very thing you've been crying out for.

Since I became a wife and mom, I've walked through more joy and also more pain than I had ever experienced before. My mom had always said that the more you love, the more opportunities there are to fear, and I find that to be more true every day. When you get married, you feel like your whole heart lives in the chest of another person, and then you have a child, and it's just like that all over again. Only now, your heart is in the chests of two people. And everywhere those people go that you love so deeply, it's like you go too. You carry them with you everywhere you go, and they carry you with them wherever they go.

There is a depth of love that cannot be put into words, and I think that is why Jesus chose to die. He knew He couldn't just say it, even though His words were perfect. He knew what He wanted to say could only be truly said by physically and completely emptying Himself out before us. He didn't feel like words alone could hold the depth, the width, and the height of the capacity of love He has for us. So in order to show us how much, He chose something even more powerful than words. He lived His life to lay it down so that you, the one that He loves, can truly live again.

He lived His life to lay it down so that you, the one that He loves, can truly live again.

As I've walked this journey for the last two years of motherhood and as I've experienced both the life of my daughter and the life of my son, who is with Jesus, there have been moments where the depth of my love for them feels so all-consuming and overwhelming. As a mother, I have no doubt that I would do anything for my children; it's not even a question. And as I've pondered and sat in this overwhelming love I have for my children, I've felt the love of my Father saying to me, "Laney, this is how I love you."

Some of the moments I have felt this overwhelming and tangible love of my Father have been in moments that I would've never expected. To be completely honest, the moments I have felt most loved have surprisingly been in the moments of my deepest pain. And I'm someone who, for most of her life, tried to avoid pain. But the way He has stepped into my pain has changed my entire view of life and my understanding of His love.

> **To be completely honest, the moments I have felt most loved have surprisingly been in the moments of my deepest pain.**

God is good. I can tell you that without a single doubt in my mind. God is faithful. I can also tell you that without a single doubt in my heart. But there have been seasons of my life that I could not have written that on paper. There have been seasons where I've felt like I've sat in the back seat, waiting to see if the next stop still shows me His faithfulness. Because when we go through pain and heartbreak, the enemy loves to try and make you believe that God isn't who He said He is.

When our baby boy went to heaven, it was so unexpected. And in the middle of the night, I spent many hours processing and asking all the "why" questions. Although I still don't have all the answers to those questions, I have seen Him take the greatest pain I'd ever known and breathe life through it, into every part of me. I'm not the same person that I was before I had the joy of mothering my son. And if I was given a choice to carry him for those 17 weeks with the very same outcome, you know there is no doubt that I would choose him all over again. Though I don't experience his life in the same way that I experience my daughter's life, because of Jesus and the hope of heaven we have, I'm still experiencing his life, just in a different way.

Before my son went to be with Jesus, I had a friend text me an encouraging word she felt for his life. She said, "Rory will be a fisher of men." This troubled me after what happened because I had taken these words to heart. I imagined Rory telling people how much Jesus loved them. Until one day, I heard the Holy Spirit say to me, "Laney, that is what he is doing through you talking about him."

To simply look at Rory's life as though I lost him is not true in light of what we know about heaven. And though I don't hold Rory like I hold my daughter, Rhonny, I think of him every time I get in my car and feel the overwhelming love of Jesus for me. Every time I feel the tangible presence of my Father with me, I think of my son. Because carrying him into heaven was one of the deepest joys, deepest pains, and greatest honors I've ever known. Being his mom has been both an earthly and heavenly experience. And what I have experienced through both my earthly pain as a mother and the overwhelming shalom of my Father is why I'm writing these words to you right now. Rory's life is speaking, just differently than I had imagined.

God's love will surprise you with how it can completely change your mind.

God's love will surprise you with how it can completely change your mind. His love can rewrite a story for you — the narrative you've always known — God's love can change how you see that story. Oftentimes, pain is what brings us to the end of ourselves. Oftentimes, pain is what causes us to throw in the towel or throw our hands up because we're all out of ideas. There have been many moments in my life where I can recall thinking, "God, I don't know how You're going to make this good." The pain is so deep. The outcome feels so final. There have been moments where I could have never imagined how in the world He could make a situation good, including the life of Rory. But I can tell you today that once again, God is God. And He has made all things good for my momma heart and my daughter's heart. And I don't hang my hat on anything less than His goodness. If it's not good, then He's just not done yet.

. . . as His daughter, I believe there is a place your Father wants to take you.

I say all this to say that, as His daughter, I believe there is a place your Father wants to take you. A journey He wants to lead you on. An adventure of discovering the wonders of His love for you. And your journey will be unique. Your story isn't meant to look exactly like mine or anyone else's, but it will wonderfully look like your own.

Your own discovery of how good and how faithful your loving Father is to you. Through joy and excitement, through questions and pain, He wants to go through it all with you. And He doesn't just want to go, but He wants to lead you. He wants to lead you by peace, while you get to follow behind with childlike wonder and expectation of good. Because though there may be moments you didn't see coming, when you're with Him, you'll find everything you're longing for and live your life completely satisfied.

> . . . when you're with Him, you'll find everything you're longing for and live your life completely satisfied.

I sat with a friend recently who walked with me through the pain of saying goodbye to Rory. She was there for me when I needed someone to talk to or someone to help me get my mind off of things. Just a few months after, she told me she was pregnant. And we rejoiced together. A few months later, she experienced the pain that I did. Saying goodbye way too soon. But as I sat with her, processing and grieving, we both sat and just wept together. And as tears kept coming, something stood out to me within my own heart. I was not crying for me. I was not crying because of my own pain, but I was crying from the pain that I knew my friend was experiencing. Because I knew that pain full and well. And just then, the words "rejoice with those who rejoice and weep with those who weep" (Romans 12:15) came to mind. Before Rory, I wouldn't have been able to sit there and know the pain that my friend was feeling. I could not have truly wept with her like I could now. And there was something heavenly about getting to weep with her. Because I knew both the pain and the healing and hope that await her in the days to come. I knew that this pain was not forever, and I knew that even when it seems impossible, God can make anything good.

Many people will say the Christian life is not rainbows and butterflies. They will tell you that the Christian life is not a promise of a good life. And though I think I know what they mean, I also have to object to the message that can send. No, God does not promise us a life without pain. And though it hasn't always looked like rainbows and butterflies, life is often like a caterpillar and a storm. And one day, the caterpillar turns into a beautiful butterfly. And one day, the storm is moved into the sea, and all we see is a rainbow, the promise of His goodness and faithfulness to us.

Even through your pain, you have a story to tell of His goodness. Even through what feels like loss, somehow God can make it the greatest gift

> **Even through your pain, you have a story to tell of His goodness.**

you've received. People will look at you like you're crazy. The world will not be able to explain the joy that radiates off of your face and pours out of your mouth. But the spirit of your loving Father can do even the most seemingly impossible things with your greatest pain.

After I gave birth to Rhonny, I experienced fear and darkness like I never had before. There were moments when I wouldn't go to sleep because the enemy had told me I might not wake up. There were moments that I asked God questions that I never imagined myself asking. Questions of His character. Questions of if He really is who He says He is, because quite honestly, I felt like He left me. There were moments that I remember feeling such excruciating physical pain and telling God that He couldn't possibly be that good if He would let me go through that. But I was honest with Him. As honest as I would be if I sat across my best friend at lunch or my dad at the dinner table. I was raw with my questions and raw with my feelings, without holding anything back. And it's wild now to think that I was once there. I'm not sure what prompted this, but I remember asking God, "If You really never leave me or forsake me, where were You then?" Specifically, I began naming moments of pain and saying, "Show me where You were in that moment." And as I asked, I can honestly tell you that each time He showed me exactly where He was, and it was always right beside me. And every time He answered my questions, somehow it led to Him being even more faithful and good than I thought.

Daughter, you might feel like you're the caterpillar right in the middle of a huge storm, but you cannot forget that the caterpillar turns into a beautiful butterfly, and it's after the storm that comes the rainbow. God has good plans for you. He has healing, better than before, awaiting you. If you find yourself in the same place that I once did and you just can't get over a certain moment or memory of pain, just simply ask Him to show you where He was in that moment. And I believe by asking this, you will see His goodness towards you. One day you will look back and barely believe that you once lived in such heartache.

The law pointed
out our need for
a savior, and then
God sent a *savior*.

Chapter 14
Tis So Sweet

When I looked in the mirror, I couldn't tell a difference. I had gotten so used to the reflection that, to me, it was normal. But my family was concerned. My friends were worried about me. It was obvious that I wasn't eating enough.

Up until about 10 years old, I didn't think much about the way I looked. There were moments I would compare myself to other girls my age, but it was not a way of life until I was about 13. Things really started to change without me even realizing it. My goal wasn't to be skinny, even though I got incredibly thin. My goal, without it even being a conscious thought of mine, was to just be "normal." I thought if I was thin like my friends, then I would just fit in, and more people might want to be friends with me.

I didn't realize until I was almost 15 that the devil had been lying to me and the enemy had built a stronghold in my life over the way I saw myself. And even more specifically, what I ate or, more often, didn't eat. My mind was daily consumed with what I would eat that day. I didn't want to eat too much because then I might not look "normal." My definition of "normal" at the time, was not a definition or revelation from Jesus. When I looked in the mirror, I was not looking at myself in light of being His daughter. I looked in the mirror and picked apart every little thing about myself that I could see.

There were days I remember having thoughts that I wished we just didn't have to eat, that eating wasn't a part of life, because of the mental battle I dealt with about overeating. What I ate and how I looked because of it were so attached to my worth that sometimes I wished food just didn't even exist. This is so sad to admit or think back on because I love food! All kinds of food, especially dessert! My favorite thing ever is cookie cake. I love Mexican food, sushi, Chick-fil-A! Can I get an amen?

But isn't it just like the enemy to take something that God made good and for our enjoyment and make it our enemy? The devil always twists and taints what God made for our good

But isn't it just like the enemy to take something that God made good and for our enjoyment and make it our enemy? The devil always twists and taints what God made for our good and pleasure.

and pleasure. The devil twists God's words to us. He twists God's heart toward us. He twists God's intentions for us. The enemy is always out to destroy the good things God has done in your life and steal from you the very things that were given to you for your enjoyment.

My journey with eating began to cause destruction in my life the day I started telling myself, "You can't have that, and you can't have that, and you can't have that." The law of telling myself, "You can't have that," truthfully made me only want it more. Doesn't that sound familiar?

First Corinthians 15:56 says, "The sting of death is sin, and the strength of sin is the law" (NKJV).

First Corinthians 15:56 says, *"The sting of death is sin, and the strength of sin is the law"* (NKJV). I have seen in absolutely every area of my life, this couldn't be more true. Whether it be what I eat or don't eat. What I do or don't do. What I say or don't say. The more I focus on it and tell myself, "Don't do that," the more likely I am to want to do it.

Because sin finds its strength and power in the law. The law is "don't do that, don't do that, don't do that." And the more I focus on what I shouldn't do, the more I'm focused on my sin. God gave us the law to see our desperate need for His grace and love for us. To clearly reveal to us that we could not do this life on our own. That we could not live a righteous life on our own. The law pointed out our need for a savior, and then God sent a savior.

So if the strength of sin is the law, what is the strength of our freedom? The strength of our freedom is the grace of God. For when we could not fulfill the law, Jesus fulfilled the law, and we live now and forever only by His grace. Everything you have, every ounce of breath in your lungs, every

The strength of our freedom is the grace of God.

time your heart beats another beat, it is His grace. Nothing you have is of your own doing.

I believe that the freedom Jesus died to give us is not just for part of our lives, but for absolutely every single part. Including our image. The way we look, the way we feel, and the way we see ourselves. He brings freedom and life to every single one of these areas.

This was the first time in my life that I realized no one could receive my freedom for me. No one could reach out for me or force me to believe that I could be free from the stronghold in my life. I had to receive it for myself. And I became desperate. There were months that I got so thin that you could see all my ribs and every bone in my back. Yet, even still, I couldn't see it when I looked in the mirror. I didn't realize how loud the voices were in my head because they were just a way of life. The voices were so loud and strong that they affected my vision and changed what I saw as my reality.

One night, after struggling with this for about a year, I remember just quietly saying to God, "Please take this from me." I was tired. I was starting to see that I was not living from freedom and the way I was living was not sustainable. The way I saw myself had become way too focused on myself. And I really wanted to be free. It was in that moment, I literally felt God lift a weight off of me. The burden I had been carrying and trying to keep up with was heavy. And in that moment, the peace of God and the healing touch of God touched me.

Now, that doesn't mean that I never had a thought over whether or not I should eat the cupcake again. There were moments that old thoughts came, and sometimes they came with vengeance. But when they came, it was not my own strength that kept me from acting on the thought, it was the love of Jesus that kept me. The love of my Father continuing to love me and heal me and set me free. It was not

... it was the love of Jesus that kept me.

an overnight moment, and I was never faced with the option to not eat again. We have meals three times a day, so it felt like I faced it often. But God's love for me and His grace for me, changed, renewed, and healed my mind. He restored to me the purity of the good thing He had made for my enjoyment.

At 14, I would've never imagined I could be this free as a 28-year-old. The freedom of Jesus is more powerful than any tainted or twisted thing of the enemy.

I remember, after God set me free, going back to a place where I used to spend a lot of time before I was free. A place where people knew me as an extremely thin teenager, and now I was a free, grown woman. There were thoughts and moments where I felt like I needed to almost fit back in those old clothes or put those shoes of bondage back on, but even in those moments, it was His love for me that kept me. It was not my own resistance or willpower; it was the power of His grace in my life.

It was not my own resistance or willpower; it was the power of His grace in my life.

Taste and See

Is there an area in your life that you long to be free? Maybe you've been longing for a really long time, and you've started to believe that freedom just isn't possible for you. I've been there. In fact, I know many people who have been there. And I also know many people who have been completely set free by the power of God's grace.

I grew up a Christian. I read my Bible and received life from reading it, but it wasn't until I was much older that I started to understand that the Bible consisted of a new covenant and an old covenant. I used to read my Bible cover to cover, like it was all in red letters. If it was in the Bible, I read it like a law for my life that I was to follow. Until I got older and started to realize that I had never plucked my eye out like Matthew 18:9 says: *"If your eye causes you to stumble, gouge it out and throw it away . . ."* (NIV). I started realizing that the Bible is actually full of many things

> . . . as I read my Bible, looking for Jesus in the story.

that I can't do. I also started to understand God's heart for me as I read my Bible, looking for Jesus in the story. And something clicked. All my life, I thought it was about living a good life and being good, and I was doing a pretty good job of it in my own eyes until I compared myself to the law and realized I actually couldn't do everything the law demands me to do. When I stand next to the law, I don't even stand a chance. And neither do you. None of us do. You can try your hardest and you can do your absolute best, but once you stand next to the law, you will see your desperate need for a savior too.

As much as this can seem like a downer at first, let me tell you, this is the best news of your life! This is the gospel and the whole reason Jesus came. To do for you and be for you what you could not do or be on your own. Second Corinthians 5:21 says it like this: *"For He made Him who knew no sin to be sin for us, that we might become the righteousness of God in Him"* (NKJV).

And Psalm 34:8 says, *"Taste and see that the LORD is good; blessed is the man who trusts in Him!"* (NKJV).

My husband had a moment in his life where God set him free of something he had dealt with most of his life. This was something he once believed he would have to live with forever. So I asked him the other day, "What do you feel like was the moment that truly set you free?" He said, "I tasted something better." He went on to say that it was no longer an effort to resist something; he stepped into a position of receiving something so much better. Instead of resisting moments of temptation, he began receiving God's love for him even in the midst of his weakness.

Clayton and I had different struggles, but it was the same thing that ultimately set us both free. Where I once craved affirmation from people, my soul found and tasted something so much more satisfying. The acceptance and affirmation of my Father. The unconditional love that He had for me. The fulfillment of a life that is about so much more than myself.

Many people today mistake the preaching of grace as a license to sin, but preaching grace is actually preaching the true power of Christ and His blood that was shed. There is no need for anything to be added to what Christ has done.

Daughter, His blood paid the full price for your salvation and for your freedom from addictions, bondage, and every stronghold. Whether it be an eating disorder, a mental struggle, or an area of condemnation, the freedom you're longing for is yours to simply receive by faith today.

"Daughter, because you dared to believe, your faith has healed you. Go with peace in your heart, and be free from your suffering!" (Mark 5:34, TPT).

Chapter 15
Dare to Believe

In Mark Chapter 5, there is a story of a woman who has had an issue of blood for 12 years. She had bled continually, she had endured a great deal under the care of various doctors, she had spent all she had on their treatments, and she was not getting better, but worse. She had suffered horribly until one day she found herself in the very same crowd that Jesus stood. When she heard about Jesus, she pushed through the crowd until she was able to touch His clothing. She had believed and said to herself, *"If only I may touch His clothes, I shall be made well." Immediately the fountain of blood was dried up, and she felt in her body that she was healed of the affliction* (Mark 5:28–29, NKJV).

I think if many of us were honest, we would say that sometimes we feel like this woman pushing through the crowd trying to get to Jesus. Although our crowd is not a crowd of people, our crowd is often made up of many distractions, fears, and lies that we're daily trying to press through.

There are so many things I love about this story, but one thing that cannot go unnoticed is that after having an issue for 12 years, this woman still believed just a touch could heal her. Just one touch from Jesus, and her whole body would be made well. And that day she found herself in His midst, she believed, and she did not return home unwell. This woman was healed instantly.

Twelve years is a long time. When I think about where I was 12 years ago and imagine having bled every day since then, I truly cannot imagine what this woman had been through. You may have walked through some things absolutely unimaginable to me as well. Your story may possibly be much like this woman's, and you've been suffering for many years. You may feel like you've been pressing through the crowd, just waiting for Jesus to walk by so that you could touch Him. Your suffering may feel long, hopeless, and worthy of doubt, but if I could encourage your heart today, like this woman, just believe.

When the woman touched Jesus, He turned around to the crowd and said, "Who touched Me?" He felt the power to heal pass through Him. Looking around to see who touched Him, the woman, fearing and trembling, knowing what had happened to her and that she had been healed, came down before Him and told Him the whole truth. And Jesus said to her, *"Daughter, because you dared to believe, your faith has healed you. Go with peace in your heart, and be free from your suffering!"* (Mark 5:34, TPT).

Many of us may look at this story and still think today, *If only I could touch Jesus, if only He were here, I would press through any crowd just to touch the hem of His clothing.* But I believe this day, Jesus was thinking of you and me when He responded to this woman. Notice He didn't turn around and say, "Now that you touched Me, you've been healed." But He said to her, "Daughter, because you dared to believe, *your faith* has healed you."

> **Faith in Jesus healed this woman. Faith in His name.**

Faith in Jesus healed this woman. Faith in His name. Faith in what she had heard about Him, even though she had never met Him face-to-face. She believed the good news about Jesus that had been spreading throughout her town.

When news is far off, it can be hard to believe. When we can't physically see what it is we believe, it's easy to grow tired, confused, or even just lose sight of what we know to be true. If this story is all you ever knew about Jesus and His time on earth, it could definitely seem that this woman had an advantage over us in seeing her savior face-to-face. And though we long for that day and what a beautiful day that will be, you and I have something this day that this woman, who was even healed of a twelve-year disease, did not have.

Daughter, I want to remind you again that this day, as a believer in Jesus, you have His spirit living, moving, and breathing inside of you. You are a new creation. The old has passed away, and all things under the righteous blood of your redeemer have been made new (2 Corinthians 5:17). And you are never on your own again, in this life or the one to come. For God promised us that He would not leave us as orphans, and He sent us an advocate to be with us forever (John 14:15–19).

I don't know what your life has looked like up until this moment. I cannot see through the lens through which you've seen your entire life. I'm sure you've seen brokenness, for the world we live in is broken. There is a ruler of this world, and the Bible tells us it is the evil one. I cannot promise life as a daughter means life without moments of brokenness, but God does promise that He is our healer, and He dwells in us within a broken world for our sake and to make us whole.

Faith in Jesus Heals

After my husband and I walked through the miscarriage of our son, it was heartbreaking the amount of messages I received from women who had walked a similar road and said it would never get better or easier. Many women said that every year would be just as hard. In an effort to comfort me and share their story, I was also impacted and saddened by the deep brokenness in which many women were still living. By all means, I was incredibly grateful for the intent, but something in my heart was unsettled the more and more I read.

I remember thinking, *I don't want to live broken. I don't want heartache and brokenness to be my story.* And I believe none of us do. None of us truly wants to live in sadness and brokenness for the rest of our days, yet many of us still don't realize we don't have to.

> **Wholeness and peace that Jesus gives, not as the world gives but as He gives, is where we're meant to live and dwell each day.**

Wholeness and peace that Jesus gives, not as the world gives but as He gives, is where we're meant to live and dwell each day.

One of the most wild things in my journey with Jesus is the amount of peace I experienced in the days around losing my son. I still can't put into words the kind of love I experienced from my Father. It was heavenly, it was supernatural, it was healing. Faith in Jesus healed and is continuing to heal my heart. My days are not marked by loss, but my days are marked by His faith-fulness and the joy that He gives. Faith in Jesus has carried me.

Faith is the foundation for everything, but if we don't know what to put faith in, it's easy to feel lost really quickly. But Daughter, you will never go wrong by putting your faith in Jesus. It's not just a name, but He is a person, and by putting your faith in Him, you're putting your faith in all that He is.

In the Bible, as Jesus walked the earth, we see that He was a provider (the feeding of the five thousand in Matthew 14:13–21), we see He was the healer (the woman with the issue of blood in Mark 5:25–29), we see Him be the redeemer (the woman at the well in John 4:5–30), we see Him as the advocate (the woman caught in adultery in John 8:1–11), and we see Him over and over as the personification of everything we need. Faith in Jesus is faith that will never forsake you.

> ... we see Him over and over as the personification of everything we need.

If you've made it this far in the book and you've never personally received the free gift of eternal life with Jesus, I would love to invite you into that reality right now. I don't know what your experience with faith has been, I don't know what you've been told about Jesus or what has been the example to you of what life with Jesus looks like, but I know no matter what you've walked through, experienced, heard, or seen in life, simply believing in His name can redeem every ounce of brokenness. He is the healer, the redeemer, and the friend you can count on forever, and He wants you to have the living water that flows from Him and never runs dry. There's nothing too big He can't redeem. There's no brokenness too broken for His healing touch. Life with Jesus is life with eternal hope. His love is not flakey, weird, or empty, but true love actually flows from Him. He is the only way we know true

He is the healer, the redeemer, and the friend you can count on forever, and He wants you to have the living water that flows from Him and never runs dry.

love, for He laid down His life for you and me that we might live forever.

Wherever you are today, you can receive His love for you and believe in your heart that He is your loving savior, redeemer, and friend. There is no formula or magic words or a system you have to follow, but the God of the universe chose to be a Father and a friend so that you could have a relationship with Him and all that's left for you to do is receive Him. By welcoming Jesus in your heart, you're welcoming His Holy Spirit to come and live inside of you, to redeem you of your past life and give you an entirely new life!

> ... the God of the universe chose to be a Father and a friend so that you could have a relationship with Him ...

That's all there is to it. And the Bible says, He will teach you all things, reminding you of what He has spoken. *"But the Advocate, the Holy Spirit, whom the Father will send in my name, will teach you all things and will remind you of everything I have said to you"* (John 14:26, NIV).

If you received Him in this moment or many years ago, you're forever His daughter. Nothing you could ever do or not do could take this beautiful, matchless gift away from you. His love is yours forever.

As you begin to walk under the revelation of who you truly are, I believe you will begin to see life a whole lot differently. For many years of my life, I believed in Jesus before I realized even a glimpse of what I had in His free gift and fullness of salvation. For many years, I believed in who He was, yet truthfully, I didn't know much of what He said or taught while He walked the earth. And although everything I've learned about Him has been good and life to my soul, I'm also incredibly grateful for the journey of life and the discovery of more of Him. So as you begin this new life with Jesus, don't let thoughts of regret steal from the new life He is leading you into. He wants to carry you forward, and as He carries you, you will see the past redeemed.

You may also be in a similar place right now as I once was. You may have believed in Jesus your entire life, yet in many ways, this position as "daughter" and the promise of an inheritance sounds foreign to you. I understand, but let me remind you once again that you're in a beautiful place, and it is never a bad idea to ask your Father to remind you who He is and who you are because of Him.

. . . you're in a beautiful place . . .

Like the woman with the issue of blood, I've dealt with my own issues. Though my issues haven't been the same as this woman's, I've known what faith in Jesus' name can do. I've seen Him heal my body, redeem my mind, and make whole a once very broken heart. And that is what I believe you will see Him do for you.

Jesus said in John 16:33, *"I have told you these things, so that in me you may have peace. In this world you will have trouble. But take heart! I have overcome the world"* (NIV).

Take heart! Take heart and take hold of all that is yours. It is time to dare to believe in all that you have heard about Him. That He is the way, the truth, and the life.

"Daughter, because you dared to believe, your faith has healed you. Go with peace in your heart, and be free from your suffering!" (Mark 5:34, TPT).

Take heart and take hold of all that is yours. It is time to dare to *believe* in all that you have heard about Him. That He is the way, the truth, and the life.

Scriptures to Receive

"But you are a chosen race, a royal priesthood, a holy nation, a people for his own possession, that you may proclaim the excellencies of him who called you out of darkness into his marvelous light" (1 Peter 2:9, ESV).

"Lord, you are great and worthy of the highest praise! For there is no end to the discovery of the greatness that surrounds you" (Psalm 145:3, TPT).

"But God demonstrates His own love toward us, in that while we were still sinners, Christ died for us" (Romans 5:8, NKJV).

"For I know the plans I have for you," declares the LORD, "plans to prosper you and not to harm you, plans to give you hope and a future" (Jeremiah 29:11, NIV).

"Every spiritual blessing in the heavenly realm has already been lavished upon us as a love gift from our wonderful heavenly Father, the Father of our Lord Jesus — all because he sees us wrapped into Christ. This is why we celebrate him with all our hearts!" (Ephesians 1:3, TPT).

"These things I have spoken to you, that My joy may remain in you, and that your joy may be full. This is My commandment, that you love one another as I have loved you. Greater love has no one than this, than to lay down one's life for his friends" (John 15:11–13, NKJV).

"For God so loved the world that He gave His only begotten Son, that whoever believes in Him should not perish but have everlasting life. For God did not send His Son into the world to condemn the world, but that the world through Him might be saved" (John 3:16–17, NKJV).

"As the Father loved Me, I also have loved you; abide in My love" (John 15:9, NKJV).

"Ask and it will be given to you; seek and you will find; knock and the door will be opened to you. For everyone who asks receives; the one who seeks finds; and to the one who knocks, the door will be opened" (Matthew 7:7–8, NIV).

"I love you, Yahweh, and I'm bonded to you, my strength! Yahweh, you're the bedrock beneath my feet, my faith-fortress, my wonderful deliverer, my God, my rock of rescue where none can reach me. You're the shield around me, the mighty power that saves me, and my high place. All I need to do is to call on you, Yahweh, the praiseworthy God. When I do, I'm safe and sound in you — delivered from my foes!" (Psalm 18:1–3, TPT).

"For if by the one man's offense death reigned through the one, much more those who receive abundance of grace and of the gift of righteousness will reign in life through the One, JESUS CHRIST" (Romans 5:17, NKJV).

"For He made Him who knew no sin to be sin for us, that we might become the righteousness of God in Him" (2 Corinthians 5:21, NKJV).

Sources

1. https://biblehub.com/hebrew/4284.htm

2. https://biblehub.com/hebrew/7965.htm

3. https://www.blueletterbible.org/lexicon/ h7451/niv/wlc/0-1/

4. https://biblehub.com/hebrew/309.htm

5. https://www.nicolecmullen.com/music

6. https://www.merriam-webster.com/ dictionary/insecurity

7. John Eldridge, *Waking the Dead* (Nashville, Nelson Books, and imprint of Thomas Nelson, 2016), 170

What's next?

Daughter, I hope and believe this book encouraged your heart! You might have known Jesus since you can remember, and this was simply a refreshing reminder of what's already yours. But maybe you didn't know Jesus yet and have experienced His healing touch through this book.

However you got here, I want to invite you to say these words out loud:

God, I believe you are God of the universe and my good Father. I receive your Holy Spirit and thank You that, because of Jesus, I can have a forever-relationship with You.

I receive the gift of Your peace and righteousness, freely given to me. I release any wrong belief that I'm supposed to strive to be better or live perfectly. I recognize that instead of my effort, Your grace and loving-kindness is all that I need.

Thank You, Jesus, for Your faithfulness to me today and forever.

Take Notes

_____

_____

_____

_____

_____

_____

_____

_____

_____

_____

_____

_____

_____

_____

_____

_____

_____

_____

_____

_____

Meet Laney

Laney is a wife, mom, and founder of The One He Loves, a ministry which exists so every woman can be refreshed, encouraged, and reminded of Jesus' loving-kindness towards them. Laney is known for sharing the goodness of Jesus in a way that is not just inviting but also captivating. After walking through a painful season and into a redemption story only Jesus could come up with, Laney couldn't keep the good news to herself. Today, as a worship artist, author, and speaker, Laney continues to find creative ways to share the heart of Jesus with everyone she can!

Ways to Connect

Laney

⊙ heylaneyrene   f LaneyReneR   ▶ Laney_Rene

For inquiries about speaking or leading worship, please email **info@laneyrene.com**

The One He Loves

To learn more about The One He Loves, please visit theoneheloves.org, and to join the community, follow **@theonehelovesministry** on Instagram and Like on Facebook.

For questions about worship nights, outreach, or other inquiries, please email **info@theoneheloves.org**